Praise for *How to Read Nonprofit Financial Statements*

"*How to Read Nonprofit Financial Statements: A Practical Guide* equips nonprofit board members, the senior management team, and key stakeholders with the information they need to effectively understand their organization's financial statements. Through detailed, line-by-line analysis of each part of a financial statement, the authors have created a premier source of information that is easy to understand regardless of professional background."

—**Michael Bauer**, Chief Financial Officer, World Wildlife Fund

HOW TO
READ
NONPROFIT
FINANCIAL
STATEMENTS

A PRACTICAL GUIDE

3e

Andrew Lang, CPA | William Eisig, CPA
Lee Klumpp, CPA, CGMA | Tammy Ricciardella, CPA

WILEY

Library of Congress Cataloging-in-Publication Data:

Names: Lang, Andrew S., author. | Eisig, William, author. | Klumpp, Lee, author. | Ricciardella, Tammy, author.
Title: How to read nonprofit financial statements: a practical guide/Andrew Lang, William Eisig, Lee Klumpp, Tammy Ricciardella.
Description: Third edition. | Hoboken: Wiley, 2017. | Revised edition of How to read nonprofit financial statements, 2010. | Includes index.
Identifiers: LCCN 2016055393 (print) | LCCN 2016056037 (ebook) | ISBN 9781118976692 (paperback) | ISBN 9781118976708 (pdf) | ISBN 9781118976715 (epub)
Subjects: LCSH: Nonprofit organizations—United States—Accounting. | Financial statements—United States.
Classification: LCC HF5686.N56 L36 2017 (print) | LCC HF5686.N56 (ebook) | DDC 657/.3—dc23
LC record available at https://lccn.loc.gov/2016055393

CONTENTS

PREFACE

I f you are familiar with the earlier versions of this publication, you know how valuable a resource this book is to readers of nonprofit financial statements. This updated edition of the publication has been expanded and incorporates even more information that will make this a must-have resource.

This edition has been updated to reflect the new requirements of the Financial Accounting Standards Board (FASB) Accounting Standards Update (ASU) 2016-14, *Not-for-Profit Entities (Topic 958): Presentation of Financial Statements of Not-for-Profit Entities,* which will be effective for most nonprofits for fiscal years beginning after December 15, 2017. The provisions of the ASU can be adopted early if a nonprofit chooses to do so.

The illustrations in this book are designed to provide readers with both the format of nonprofit financial statements before the adoption of ASU 2016-14 as well as the format once a nonprofit adopts the provisions of ASU 2016-14. The illustrations highlight best practices as well as the required changes outlined in the ASU. These illustrations provide a great resource for those trying to read and interpret nonprofit financial statements as well as for those who are responsible for designing and preparing nonprofit financial statements.

A new chapter has been provided that discusses reserves. This is a challenging topic and one that many organizations struggle with, and unfortunately there isn't a single, definitive answer. There are certain considerations and other factors, however, that an organization should analyze in making an assessment regarding appropriate reserves.

This edition provides a new section discussing general financial analysis that provides greater insight into what readers of nonprofit financial statements should be looking for to enable them to satisfy their fiduciary responsibility whether they are a board member, audit committee member, advisor, or internal CEO or CFO. The section also provides some of the more common ratios that can be used to obtain information about the financial condition of a nonprofit organization. This information should be used by all readers and preparers of nonprofit financial statements to ensure the financial statements are designed to provide an accurate depiction of the nonprofit organization's financial position, activities, and results.

This edition also includes a new chapter on benchmarking to assist nonprofits in making comparisons to other nonprofit organizations.

A glossary is included that will assist readers in identifying the meaning of specific terms used in nonprofit accounting and financial statements that can be referred to time and time again.

LEARNING OBJECTIVES

E very educational effort should have a specific focus. This text has been designed so that once you have completed it, you will be able to:

- Name and understand the primary purpose of a nonprofit's basic financial statements.
- Recognize best practices in the presentation of financial information in nonprofit financial statements.
- Understand the significance of the independent auditor's report and be able to recognize an unmodified (clean) opinion and other types of audit opinions.
- Understand the role of the footnotes in financial statements and the purpose they serve.
- Extract and interpret certain financial information from each of the basic financial statements.
- Understand the basic accounting rules that apply specifically to nonprofit organizations.
- Understand the new financial statement presentation changes required by ASU 2016-14.
- Understand the method of assessing the need for reserves.
- Familiarize yourself with common financial ratios that are useful in assessing the financial health of a nonprofit organization.
- Identify benchmarking techniques.
- Recognize the future complexities related to nonprofit financial reporting.

INTRODUCTION

This book is designed to help you understand the financial statements of nonprofit organizations. If you are a nonprofit executive or volunteer leader who is not familiar with the formats and language of financial reports, or if you simply wish to brush up on your skills, you will find that this book has been prepared especially for you.

Understanding financial information is vital to managing a successful nonprofit organization. As a nonprofit executive, you know this to be true. If you are a volunteer leader and wish to fulfill your fiduciary responsibility to guide your organization, it is equally important. The best leaders do not lead without this knowledge.

The text is intended to provide you with knowledge that you can apply in carrying out your roles and responsibilities in your organization. To that end, you are encouraged to work through the exercises presented to gain insight into the principal concepts surrounding nonprofit financial statements. The exercises reinforce the concepts presented.

The requirements of nonprofit financial reporting in general have grown increasingly complex over the years. The purpose of financial reporting is to provide the financial story of the organization. With the issuance of the Financial Accounting Standards Board (FASB) Accounting Standards Update 2016-14, *Not-for-Profit Entities (Topic 958): Presentation of Financial Statements of Not-for-Profit Entities,* the requirements for how information is presented in nonprofit financial statements have been significantly updated. This edition has been updated to reflect these new requirements and provides explanations and illustrations of many of the new financial statement presentation requirements.

Also, many nonprofit organizations have activities, such as significant federal funding, that require unique reports. These reports and the requirements have also changed as a result of the Office of Management and Budget issuing Title 2 Code of Federal Regulations (CFR) Part 200, *Uniform Administrative Requirements, Cost Principles, and Audit Requirements for Federal Awards* (Uniform Guidance). As a result, special materials have been added near the end of the text to provide those interested with the most important information pertaining to these activities and the updated reporting.

A glossary is included at the end of the text to familiarize you with both the common terms associated with nonprofit financial statements and to provide you with a resource for the future. Understanding the language of nonprofit organizations is essential to understanding your organization's financial statements.

By beginning to read this text, you have taken an important first step in increasing your capabilities. When you have finished the text, you will have accomplished something truly worthwhile.

CHAPTER 1

Why You Need to Understand the Update to the Nonprofit Reporting Model

Anyone who is responsible in some way for the welfare of a nonprofit organization, whether as a leader, member, donor, manager, or staff, needs to be well aware of recent changes in rules affecting all nonprofit financial reporting. The Accounting Standards Update (ASU) 2016-14 will change the way nonprofits classify net assets and prepare their financial statements. While the changes do not substantially alter a nonprofit's financial statements, they are of sufficient significance that they must be understood by those with a fiduciary responsibility or simply an interest in the well-being of the entity.

This book has been prepared for any and all readers. It provides definitions of common accounting jargon and provides numerous examples of financial statements reflecting both the old standards and the new ones. We applaud you for investing your time to understand what is new in our nonprofit world.

CHAPTER 2

Why Update the Nonprofit Reporting Model?

The current reporting model for nonprofit organizations has been in existence for more than 20 years. Many stakeholders raised the question as to whether a refreshed model would be more useful to users of nonprofit financial statements. The Financial Accounting Standards Board (FASB) analyzed the situation based on input from the nonprofit industry and concluded that improvements were in order. They then added the project Financial Statements of Not-for-Profit Entities to its agenda, which ultimately led to the issuance of Accounting Standards Update (ASU) 2016-14, *Not-for-Profit Entities (Topic 958): Presentation of Financial Statements of Not-for-Profit Entities.*

The goals of ASU 2016-14 are to improve the overall understandability, comparability, and usefulness of nonprofit financial statements. The ASU is not an overhaul but an update of existing standards for nonprofit organizations. The update to the current presentation of the net asset classification requirements is one major component of the project. Another aspect of the project was to work to improve the information provided by nonprofits to allow readers to be able to assess the liquidity, financial performance, and cash flows of nonprofit organizations.

Thus, the ASU is aimed at revising current reporting practices so that they are clarified to allow for clearer reporting on how restrictions on a nonprofit's resources affect liquidity. The ASU requires enhanced disclosures about financial assets and the extent to which they are not available in the near term because of limits imposed by donors, laws, and internal governing board actions. These expanded disclosures should assist users of nonprofit financial statements in assessing an entity's liquidity.

ASU 2016-14 affects substantially all nonprofit entities as defined in the FASB Accounting Standards Codification (ASC). Based on the ASC, nonprofit entities are defined as "an entity that possesses the following characteristics, in varying degrees, that distinguish it from a business entity: (a) contributions of significant amounts of resources from resource providers who do not expect commensurate or proportionate pecuniary return, (b) operating purposes other than to provide goods or services at a profit, and (c) absence of ownership interests like those of business entities." While the first or second characteristic may or may not apply to your organization, the third most certainly should cover the industry as a whole.

CHAPTER 3

Highlights of the Major Changes to the Nonprofit Reporting Model

Net Asset–Related Changes

Update to Net Asset Presentation

The ASU requires a change in the presentation of temporarily and permanently restricted net assets to a single classification of net assets with donor restrictions. This change is designed to reduce complexity and increase understandability of this information. The ASU also requires enhanced disclosures that show the detail of net assets with donor restrictions at the end of the reporting period as well as how the restrictions affect the use of the resources. This additional information must be presented in either the face of the statement of financial position or in the footnotes to the financial statements. The FASB believes that the expanded presentation about various types of restrictions would provide more information than the current aggregated summaries of the total temporarily and permanently restricted net assets presentation and disclosures currently provided to readers of the financial statements.

The previously categorized unrestricted net assets will now be referred to as net assets without donor restrictions. The terminology change is seen as a refinement since the use of the term *unrestricted net assets* implies that the assets are not subject to any restrictions. However this category of net assets is oftentimes subject to restrictions resulting from laws, regulations, and other terms and conditions of bond agreements and other contracts. This change in terminology will more clearly show that these net assets are not subject to any donor restrictions but can in fact be subject to restriction by these other arrangements or parties.

The presentation of net assets with donor restrictions will encompass both the categories previously titled temporarily and permanently restricted net assets with the goal of streamlining this presentation to show all assets with donor restrictions. This category includes funds received with restrictions from both donors and grantors. There has been a lot of confusion in the past surrounding the classification between temporarily and permanently restricted net assets, and this change aims to eliminate this confusion. The use of the term *with donor restrictions* is a heading, and an entity can maintain subcategories under this heading, as they feel necessary to clearly portray their net assets. The disclosures for net assets with donor restrictions should clearly state the nature, purpose, and amount of the donor restrictions so that a reader can fully understand the nature of the restrictions.

Disclosures of Board-Designated Net Assets

The ASU requires additional information to be disclosed either on the face of the statement of financial position or in the notes to the financial statements regarding the various types of board-designated net assets. These are net assets without donor restrictions that the nonprofit's board imposes limits on for specified purposes. This change will assist nonprofit entities in showing how they are managing their resources. The purpose of the board-designated net assets is now required to be disclosed in the footnotes. The FASB also believes this will help nonprofit entities clarify their financial condition and results.

Update to Presentation of Underwater Endowments

Under the ASU, the amount that a donor-restricted endowment fund is underwater will now be presented as part of net assets with donor restrictions. The term *underwater endowments* refers to the situation in which the fair value of the assets to be maintained in perpetuity measured at the financial statement date is less than the original gift or the level required to be maintained by the donor stipulation or law. The premise for the change in showing the underwater amounts as part of net assets with donor restrictions instead of as net assets without donor restrictions is due to changes in the enacted version of the Uniform Prudent Management of Institutional Funds Act (UPMIFA) that allows spending, within the guidelines of prudence, from an underwater endowment fund. The FASB believes that the presentation of the entire amount of an endowment fund as donor restricted, whether underwater or not, is consistent with current laws. FASB also believes that keeping the full endowment in one place reduces the complexity of this information and thereby makes the information on endowment funds easier to understand.

The disclosures related to underwater endowments will continue to include the aggregate amounts by which funds are underwater as in current accounting principles generally accepted in the United States of America (U.S. GAAP). The disclosures, however, will also include the aggregate of the original gift amounts for such funds, fair value, and any governing board policy or decision to reduce or not spend from these funds.

Expirations of Capital Restrictions

The ASU will require that nonprofits use the placed-in-service approach to recognize gifts of cash restricted for acquisition or construction of property, plant, and equipment in the absence of a specific donor stipulation to the contrary. This change will assist in reducing the diversity in practice currently seen in nonprofit financial statements. Before the ASU, a nonprofit could recognize a gift over the implied time restriction related to the gift and recognize revenue as they depreciated the asset if this was their policy. Upon adoption of ASU 2016-14, this option has been eliminated unless the donor specifically states a period of time that the contributed asset must be used. This is the only provision in the ASU that changes the accounting (recognition and measurement). All other provisions in the ASU are presentation changes only.

Expense Reporting–Related Changes

Nonprofits will be required to provide an analysis of expenses that shows expenses detailed by nature and by function. Nonprofits have the option to present this information in the statement of activities, a separate statement, or in the footnotes. If the entity chooses to present the analysis in a separate statement, it must be presented as part of the basic financial statements and cannot be presented as a supplemental schedule to the financial statements. The analysis component requires that expenses be shown disaggregated by function and nature. Most nonprofits are currently required to show expenses by function either on the face of the statement of activities or in the footnotes. Currently under U.S. GAAP, only voluntary health and welfare organizations are required to include a separate statement of functional expenses that shows expenses by function and natural classification. Under the ASU all nonprofit entities will be required to provide this analysis of expenses.

Organizations may want to take this opportunity to revisit how they have defined their programs (functions) and assess whether any activities should be combined. If an entity has a large number of programs, the analysis of expenses may become over-whelming to the readers of the financial statements.

Nonprofits will also be required to provide disclosures about the methods they use to allocate costs among the program and supporting services. None of the changes in the ASU with regard to the allocation of expenses changes U.S. GAAP related to the accounting for and disclosure of joint cost activities.

Investment Return–Related Changes

To address issues with diversity in practice with the comparability of the investment return presentation, the ASU will now require nonprofits to present only the net investment return on the face of the statement of activities. The investment expenses that should be netted against investment return are limited to external investment expenses incurred and direct internal investment expenses. External investment expenses are those that are reported to the nonprofit by their external money managers and other external investment management firms related to the management of the investment portfolio. *Direct internal investment expenses* are defined in the ASU as those that "involve the direct conduct or supervision of the strategic and tactical activities involved in generating investment return." These can include, but are not limited to, salaries of officers, and other staff responsible for the development and execution of the investment strategy and allocable costs associated with internal investment management and supervising of the external investment firms. Direct internal investment expenses do not include items that are not associated with generating investment return such as accounting staff costs associated with reconciling and recording investment transactions.

The amount of investment expenses will no longer be required to be disclosed. The disclosure of investment income components, such as interest and dividends, realized gains or losses, and unrealized gains or losses, will also no longer be required in the footnotes. If the presentation of this information is still seen as useful by an entity, however, it can choose to continue to disclose this information.

Liquidity and Availability

The ASU requires new disclosures to assist readers in assessing a nonprofit's liquidity and providing information on the availability of the nonprofit's assets to meet operating needs. A nonprofit will be required to disclose qualitative information (i.e., lines of credit and reserves) on how the entity manages its liquid available resources and its liquidity risk in their footnotes. A nonprofit will also have to provide quantitative information that communicates the availability of the entity's current financial assets on the date of their statement of financial position to meet the cash needs for general expenditures within one year of the date of the statement of financial position. The information on the availability of assets can be presented on the face of the financial statements or can be disclosed in the footnotes.

Operating Measure

The ASU provides for some additional disclosures for those nonprofits that currently present an operating measure in the statement of activities and show governing board designations, appropriations, and similar actions such as internal transfers in this measure. The nonprofits with these scenarios must report these types of internal transfers appropriately disaggregated and described by type. This information can be provided either on the face of the financial statements or in the footnotes. This is designed to assist readers of the financial statements in understanding the impact these designations, appropriations, and transfers have on the operating measure presented.

Cash Flow Statement

The ASU will continue to permit nonprofits to choose between using the direct method or the indirect method of presentation for the cash flow statement. The direct method reports major classes of gross cash receipts and gross cash payments in the statement. The indirect method reports information related to the cash activities by adjusting the change in net assets for all noncash transactions and the changes in the assets and liabilities of the entity.

If an entity chooses to use the direct method of presentation, the separate reconciliation between the net change in net assets to cash flows from operating activities is required under current U.S. GAAP. The ASU will no longer require this reconciliation for those entities that choose the direct method of presentation.

Summary of Provisions

A nonprofit is permitted to incorporate many of these changes in its financial statements without adopting the full ASU.

An entity can implement the following provisions of the ASU at any point before the formal adoption:

a. Expand disclosure of board-designated net assets
b. Adjust the use of the placed-in-service approach for the recognition of revenue related to gifts of cash restricted for acquisition or construction of property, plant, or equipment
c. Present the analysis of expenses by nature and function and expanded disclosures related to the allocation methodology used by the entity
d. Present the disclosures regarding liquidity and availability of financial assets

A nonprofit can implement the following provisions of the ASU only upon adoption of the full ASU:

a. Present only one class of restricted net assets
b. Adopt the change in accounting for underwater endowments
c. Eliminate disclosure of investment return components while showing only the netted investment return number
d. Eliminate the presentation of the indirect reconciliation in the statement of cash flows if using the direct method for presenting operating cash flows

ASU Provisions with an Accounting Effect

The main provisions of the ASU address the presentation of information in nonprofit financial statements and the related disclosures regarding certain items. Two changes mandated in the ASU that could have a potential accounting effect on the financial information presented are as follows:

a. Change from using the placed-in-service approach to recognize revenue from funds received to acquire or construct property, plant, or equipment. If the entity has been recognizing revenue as the asset that was acquired or constructed is depreciated, the entity will have to discontinue this practice. The effect of capitalizing and recognizing revenue as of the date the asset was actually placed-in-service could have an effect on the financial statements presented and require an adjustment to be made retroactively to reflect this change.
b. The change in the calculation and presentation of net investment return because this now includes direct internal investment expenses.

If entities have these scenarios, they have to calculate the effect on the earliest financial period presented and adjust the financial statements for the financial impact in all periods presented in the financial statements.

Effective Date of ASU

ASU 2016-14 will be effective for nonprofit organizations' financial statements for fiscal years beginning after December 15, 2017, and for interim periods within fiscal years beginning after December 15, 2018. This means that all nonprofits with calendar year-ends will have to present their financial statements in accordance with the ASU for the first time in their December 31, 2018, financial statements. Nonprofits with fiscal year-ends would need to present their financial statements in accordance with the ASU for their respective year-ends in 2019. An entity has an option to adopt the provisions of the ASU early. If an entity chooses to adopt the provisions of the ASU early, they must apply all the provisions of the ASU in their statements presented in the year of adoption.

When an entity adopts the provisions of the ASU, it should be done on a retrospective basis for all years presented. This means that the changes in the ASU need to be applied to both the earlier year(s) and the current year presented in the financial statements. However, if an entity presents comparative financial statements that show an earlier year, the organization would have an option to omit the following information for any years presented before the year of adoption:

• Analysis of expenses by both functional and natural classification
• Disclosures around liquidity and availability of resources

If this option is selected, the analysis of expenses and the disclosures of liquidity and availability of resources would have to be shown in the financial statements only for the year the ASU is adopted. If the nonprofit shows comparative financial statements, these items should be presented for all future financial statements for both years presented in years after adoption if the entity chooses to present a comparative financial statement.

The full ASU can be accessed on FASB's website at www.fasb.org.

CHAPTER 4

What Is the Purpose of Financial Statements?

Financial statements should provide a summary of the nonprofit organization's financial position and its activities. The statements should tell the reader the story of how the organization fulfilled its mission or strategic plan and fulfilled the needs of its members, stakeholders, those in need of its services, or benefit from its services. Each nonprofit organization has a story to tell, and the financial statements should facilitate this communication.

Users of nonprofit financial statements vary in their nature, depending on the type of organization they work with. Each of these users, however, should be able to obtain the information about the resources received and available for use and how those resources were used that he or she is looking for from the financial statements. Members of a trade association should be able to see how the association was funded and what services it provided that benefited its members. Donors to a charitable organization should be able to see the resources provided to the charity and assess how their donation was used to satisfy the mission of the charity. Thus, regardless of the nature of the nonprofit organization, the financial statements should allow the interested stakeholders to assess the nonprofit's impact and whether they want to support the entity.

CHAPTER 5

Types of Financial Statements

There are two major types of financial statements. The most common type is an internal financial statement. It is created by the organization's accounting staff and is intended for the use of management, volunteer leaders, and boards of directors. Internal financial statements are usually produced each month. These internal statements are not always prepared with all the information required by accounting principles generally accepted in the United States of America (U.S. GAAP), as internal financial statements serve a different purpose from external financial statements.

The other type of financial statements are audited financial statements. These financial statements are also prepared by the nonprofit's financial staff, almost always as of the end of an organization's fiscal year. Once the document is prepared, however, it is handed over to the organization's independent external auditors, who must carefully examine it to make sure that it is reasonably accurate and complies with an exhaustive set of accounting rules governing what a nonprofit reports and how it must be reported.

Both types of financial statements are discussed later in the materials. The text, however, focuses largely on audited financial statements prepared in conformity with U.S. GAAP that, by definition, must reflect current industry accounting standards. The external audited financial statements must include the following three basic financial statements:

1. The *Statement of Financial Position* (or *Balance Sheet*) shows what the assets (things of value) and liabilities (debts) of the nonprofit were at a given point in time.
2. The *Statement of Activities* (or *Income Statement*) shows what comprised the revenue and expenses of the operations for a given period of time (usually one year) and whether there was an increase or decrease in the net assets of the organization.
3. The *Statement of Cash Flows* demonstrates where the organization's cash came from and how the cash was used.

Once an organization adopts ASU 2016-14, it may also have a *Statement of Functional Expenses* (although the title may vary) that presents an analysis of expenses by nature and function. Under ASU 2016-14, the presentation of this analysis of expenses is required. The audit committee (or those charged with governance), however, will have the option of presenting this detail as a separate basic financial statement, in the statement of activities, or in the footnotes to the financial statements.

The audited financial statements may also include the following financial statements, but they are not required.

1. The *Statement of Changes in Net Assets* is used by nonprofits to provide information on the changes in each class of net assets. It generally shows the opening balance of net assets, adds or subtracts the net change in net assets for the year (the change in net assets is calculated by adding the revenue and gains and subtracting the expenses and losses), and then shows the ending balance of net assets.
2. The *Statement of Functional Expenses* shows a detailed breakdown of expenses by expense type (for example, salaries, rent, and so forth) and by program and supporting services. This statement is currently *required* only for voluntary health and welfare organizations.

However, as already noted, upon adoption of the provisions of ASU 2016-14, all nonprofit organizations will be required to show an analysis of expenses by natural and functional classifications. Entities will have the option under ASU 2016-14 to show this analysis in the statement of activities, in the footnotes, or as a separate basic financial statement (i.e., statement of functional expenses). This presentation cannot be included as supplemental information to the financial statements to meet the requirement under ASU 2016-14.

CHAPTER 6

How to Read a Nonprofit Financial Statement

When you read a financial statement, take a systematic approach.

First, *check the heading* that is required to be included at the top of every page. Headings will tell you what organization, or group of organizations, is the subject of the report. The headings will tell you the type of statement that is being provided and the relevant measurement date (for the Statement of Financial Position) or period of time (for the Statement of Activities, Statement of Functional Expenses, and Statement of Cash Flows) that is covered by the statement. The Statement of Financial Position is a snapshot of the organization's assets, liabilities, and net assets at a particular point in time, while the Statement of Activities shows the financial activity for a period of time ending on a particular date. The Statement of Cash Flows shows the sources and uses of cash for a period of time ending on a particular date. The Statement of Functional Expenses shows the analysis of expenses by natural and functional classifications for a period of time ending on a particular date.

Second, *look for comparative data*. For a Statement of Financial Position, you will usually be provided the organization's financial position at the same time in the prior year. For the Statement of Activities, you will usually be given information for the same period of time in the prior year (or possibly "this month" versus "year to date"). The most recent data are usually shown first.

Third, *scan the page as a whole*. Most statements are shown complete on one page. Once you understand the major components of the statement, you can work more confidently on the detail in each section.

CHAPTER 7

Statement of Financial Position

The Statement of Financial Position (Balance Sheet) is usually divided into two major categories, with assets listed first and liabilities and net assets detailed below.

If the leaders of an entity want to present what is referred to as a classified Statement of Financial Position, they would show categories for current and long-term assets and liabilities separately. Assets that are expected to be used within the 12-month time horizon following the fiscal year end are considered current assets. All other assets are considered to be long-term or noncurrent assets. Liabilities that are expected to be paid within the 12-month time horizon following the fiscal year end would be considered current liabilities. All other liabilities are classified as long-term or noncurrent liabilities.

In a classified Statement of Financial Position, assets are then presented in sub-categories—current assets (cash or assets that can be converted to cash within a year) and noncurrent assets—by order of liquidity. This classified presentation is not required, so you may also see statements that present only listings of assets and liabilities with no breakdown of current and noncurrent items. However, assets and liabilities are required to be displayed in the Statement of Financial Position in order of liquidity for assets and in order of maturity for liabilities. The footnotes may contain additional information to assess liquidity.

With the adoption of ASU 2016-14, nonprofit organizations may choose to list their assets and liabilities by current and noncurrent classifications to assist in satisfying the new quantitative liquidity disclosure requirements. There are also new quantitative and qualitative disclosures regarding liquidity that are required which will assist readers in assessing liquidity.

Noncurrent assets include fixed assets, such as property, plant (buildings), equipment, and other assets that are neither fixed nor current (for example, deposits paid to the telephone company). Liabilities and net assets are then usually divided into current liabilities (debts to be paid within a year), long-term liabilities, and net assets (or net worth).

Pre-ASU 2016-14, there are three classes of net assets: unrestricted, temporarily restricted, and permanently restricted. These classifications inform you of whether or not there are any donor-imposed restrictions on the use of these net assets and if there are restrictions, the nature and timing of those restrictions. Unrestricted net assets result from excess revenues over expenses (net income) that have accumulated over the years, or from contributions from third parties that are available to be used in any way allowed by the organization's exempt status. Temporarily restricted net assets have limitations set by the donor as to how they may be used. There are two types of temporarily restricted net assets: *purpose restricted*, such as for a particular project or program, and *time restricted*, such as by the end of the next fiscal year. Some net assets may be both purpose and time restricted. Permanently restricted net assets have limitations set by the donors that impose restrictions on funds that stipulate resources be maintained permanently but often permits the nonprofit organization to use up or expend part or all of the income or other economic benefits derived from the donated assets. Donors may permit organizations to use any income or other economic benefits earned from the donated assets for general operations or they may restrict these funds to a specified purpose.

Upon the implementation of ASU 2016-14, the net assets will be presented in only two classes: without donor restriction and with donor restriction. This change has been made to make it easier for readers of the financial statements to understand which assets of the entity have restrictions placed on them by external parties and which do not have any restrictions. There was confusion in the nonprofit industry with regard to what is referred to as *unrestricted net assets*. This term was used to refer to the fact that there were no donor-imposed restrictions on these net assets.

There could be other restrictions, however, placed on these funds by lenders or others. Using the term *unrestricted* implied no restrictions at all, when in fact, nonprofits may have funds that are restricted in regard to their use by outside parties other than donors.

Steps to Analyze the Statement of Financial Position

As you look at the numbers on the Statement of Financial Position, locate the various totals and subtotals. A single underline usually indicates a subtotal, and a double underline usually indicates a grand total. As the name implies, a properly constructed Statement of Financial Position, or Balance Sheet, always shows the assets to be equal to the liabilities plus the net assets.

The Statement of Financial Position can tell you a lot about an organization's financial strength and stability, but you need to know what to look for. Have the current assets increased or decreased? If they have changed, how does this change compare to the change in the current liabilities? This will help you decide how well an organization is able to pay its bills and current expenses. Have any major fixed assets been purchased or sold? Has any new debt been taken on, or old debt paid off? Determine whether cash increases are from earnings or from borrowings. Do you notice any unusual liabilities? If so, what are they? If the statement is comparative, how has the organization changed during the time period involved in comparison to the prior year? These and similar questions will be raised and answered in the examples included later on in the text.

CHAPTER 8

Statement of Activities

The Statement of Activities presents revenues and gains and then expenses and losses as two separate major categories.

Revenues are inflows of assets that result from the entity's ongoing major or central operations and activities. Revenues are shown by type, and then totaled. Revenues are usually grouped by type or service. Not all nonprofit organizations have the same sources of revenue or the sources may be grouped differently based on their relative importance. Gains are increases in net assets resulting from an entity's peripheral or incidental transactions and other events and circumstances affecting the entity other than those that result from revenues. Peripheral or incidental transactions are those that are not an integral part of the entity's usual activities or those not significant to the annual budget. Gains can result from the change in the value of assets held, as well as transactions such as a sale of a building or a favorable outcome from a lawsuit.

Expenses are outflows of assets or incurrences of liabilities that result from an entity's ongoing major or central operations and activities. Expenses are often shown by program type, and then totaled.

The difference between revenue and expenses is the change in net assets. The change in net assets is also referred to by some as the bottom line.

Losses are decreases in net assets from an entity's peripheral or incidental transactions and other events or circumstances affecting the entity other than those that result from expenses. Losses can result from a decrease in the value of assets held as well as transactions such as natural disasters or the sale of a building or loss of a lawsuit. All said, revenue, expenses, gains and losses should be grouped by homogenous categories. Items that are substantially different should be shown separately.

The change in net assets or bottom-line figure is added to the beginning net assets to arrive at the ending net assets. This is often shown at the bottom of the Statement of Activities. When this format is used, you should make sure that the net assets reported on the Statement of Activities agree with the net assets on the Statement of Financial Position. Other times, this can be presented separately in a Statement of Changes in Net Assets. In this case be sure the net assets reported here agree with the Statement of Financial Position and that the bottom line also agrees with the Statement of Activities. It is also wise to trace the opening net assets of the current year's statements to the ending net assets of the prior year's financial statements. These are measures to test that the financial statements are constructed correctly.

The Statement of Activities also provides information about the revenue received and expenditures made with donor-imposed restrictions. The presentation of the receipt and disbursement of restricted net assets can be made in one of two ways, either a columnar or layered format on the Statement of Activities. A columnar format presents each class of net assets in a separate column. The layered format presents each class of net assets in a separate section of the statement as you work your way down the page.

Making matters even more complex is the fact that expenditures are required to be presented as decreases in unrestricted net assets (or after implementation of ASU 2016-14, net assets without donor restrictions). Since expenditures are shown as decreases in unrestricted net assets, when an entity uses restricted resources to fund activities, there needs to be a movement of restricted funds to offset these expenses. As a result, when expenditures are made with restricted resources, an amount equal to the amount of the expenditure is presented as a simultaneous decrease in temporarily restricted net assets (or after implementation of ASU 2016-14, net assets with donor restrictions) and an increase in unrestricted net assets (net assets without donor restrictions), with the description "net assets released from restriction." This reclassification mechanism is how the restricted resources are moved to the unrestricted column to offset the expenses. The net effect is that unrestricted net assets (net assets without donor restriction) are increased and decreased by the same amount, while the restricted assets simply are reduced.

The Statement of Activities frequently summarizes detailed information that is available by department, or program, within the organization. Most organizations split their activities into departments or divisions based on their programs. Separate departmental statements may be presented in internal financial statements for internal management purposes.

Steps to Analyze the Statement of Activities

The Statement of Activities offers valuable information about an organization's operating results. Compare this period's bottom line to the prior period. Then consider the various items that have affected the bottom line. Have the gross revenues and support gone up or down? Have the sources of revenue changed? What are the key sources of revenue, and have they gone up or down? What about expenses? Have total expenses gone up or down? How does the change in expenses relate to the change in revenue? Which individual expenses have changed significantly?

Some organizations choose to present operating and nonoperating sections on their Statement of Activities. The entity will define what activities are deemed to be part of operations and those that are deemed to be nonoperating based on the nature of the activities. If an organization chooses to present an operating measure, then the organization is required to disclose in the footnotes how the organization defines operating and nonoperating if this isn't clearly outlined in the Statement of Activities. The operating section would contain all activities an organization carries out as part of their mission or main purpose. The nonoperating section would contain those sources of revenue, expenses, gains, and losses that are not considered directly related to the organization's mission and are often activities that cannot be directly controlled by the organization.

If an organization chooses to segregate operating and nonoperating items, one section of the Statement of Activities will include all the income and expenses that are considered as being from operations, with a subtotal of excess revenue over expenses (surplus) or excess expenses over revenue (deficit) from operations. Following that subtotal will be a second section titled "Nonoperating." This section will include revenue, expenses, gains, and losses that the organization does not consider part of the operations of the organization. Nonprofit organizations are prohibited from using language such as net income or operating income. Many organizations will consider all or part of the investment return nonoperating and report this separately in this section in the Statement of Activities. The effect of this presentation is to eliminate such things as investment return fluctuations or other items that cause volatility in the Statement of Activities, which are not within the control of management, from operating results.

After adoption of ASU 2016-14, if an organization presents an operating measure and shows governing board designations, appropriations, and similar actions in the non-operating section, the entity will be required to report these types of transactions appropriately disaggregated and described by type either on the face of the financial statements or in the footnotes. The addition of this information will aid readers in understanding how these types of transactions affected the entity's financial position during the period covered in the financial statements.

CHAPTER 9

Statement of Cash Flows

The Statement of Cash Flows provides relevant and useful information about cash receipts and cash disbursements during a period of time. This statement helps creditors and others assess the organization's ability to generate positive future cash flows and to meet its obligations and its need for external financing. There are three important and distinctive metrics in the Statement of Cash Flows. The three metrics include cash provided by or used in operating, investing, and financing activities of the entity. As a reader of the financial statements, check to see how these metrics compare with your expectations based on the internal financial reports provided throughout the year by management and the approved budget.

Cash flows from operating activities can be thought of as the excess (or deficit) of cash revenues from operations over cash expenses from operations. It is important to note, however, that based on the definition for financial reporting purposes, cash flow from operating activities is defined as everything that is not investing or financing. Cash flows from investing activities consist of cash increases, such as those from the sale of fixed assets or investments, and cash decreases, such as those involved in purchasing fixed assets or investments. Cash flows from financing activities include increases in cash from borrowing on a line-of-credit or other loans and decreases in cash from loan repayments.

Entities have the option of presenting the Statement of Cash Flows on the direct method or the indirect method. The direct method presents items that directly affected cash flows and shows the cash receipts and payments. There is no adjustment for noncash expenses such as depreciation in this presentation. As a result, if you use the direct method, a separate schedule reconciling the net change in net assets to net cash flows from operating activities must be provided. The indirect method is an alternative presentation. In this presentation, the net cash provided by operating activities is derived by adjusting operating activities for revenue and expense items that did not result from cash transactions. The direct method is preferred by the Financial Accounting Standards Board although the indirect method of presentation is more widely used.

Upon adoption of ASU 2016-14, entities will still have the option to present the Statement of Cash Flows on the direct or indirect method. If an entity chooses to use the direct method of presentation, however, the separate reconciliation between the net change in net assets to cash flows from operating activities will no longer be required.

This change was incorporated in an effort to increase the use of the direct method of presentation.

Steps to Analyze the Statement of Cash Flows

Use the Statement of Cash Flows to find out how an organization obtained its cash and how it used it. Look at the organization's cash position at both the beginning and the end of the accounting period. As the most liquid asset of all, cash plays an important role in maintaining an organization's financial health and stability. Sufficient cash, along with the ability to readily convert other assets into cash, is important for maintaining an organization's financial liquidity and flexibility.

When you read a Statement of Cash Flows, pay attention to the bottom line of this statement: the net increase or decrease in cash. Then look at the three individual metrics (operating, investing, and financing) and identify the separate items contributing to the change. If cash has increased considerably, note whether it came from operations (that is, the day-to-day activities of the organization) or from an investing or financing activity. For example, an organization can have negative net cash flows from operations and still have working capital because it has just received cash on its line-of-credit—a cash inflow from a financing activity. If an organization is constantly using the line-of-credit, however, a reader must question why. There are many logical answers, including using the line-of-credit to offset the timing or seasonality of cash flows. This can also, however, be an indicator of potential cash flow problems.

With the adoption of ASU 2016-14, an organization will continue to have the option to present the Statement of Cash Flows under the direct or indirect method. A large percentage of organizations currently follow the indirect method. A preferred method, however, is to use the direct method. Under the direct method, the Statement of Cash Flows presents the same categories of cash flows from operating activities, investing activities, and financing activities, but the presentation of the operating activities is depicted by showing the sources and uses of cash such as cash received from contributors. Under the ASU, if an entity chooses to use the direct method, it no longer has to provide the reconciliation of the change in net assets to cash from operating activities. It is important to note that the direct method is easier for users, especially board members, to understand.

CHAPTER 10

Statement of Functional Expenses

In some financial statements, a Statement of Functional Expenses is presented. This statement presents expenses of the organization in a matrix format by both the functional basis (that is, programs such as membership, conferences, and supporting services such as general and administrative) and on a natural basis (that is, salaries or rent). Before the adoption of ASU 2016-14, this statement was required to be presented only by voluntary health and welfare organizations. All other nonprofit organizations currently have the option to present this statement, and they have the option of presenting this as a basic statement or as a supplemental schedule to the basic financial statements.

As noted previously, after the adoption of ASU 2016-14, an analysis of expenses by nature and function will be required by all nonprofit organizations. Under ASU 2016-14, the entity has a choice in how to present this information. An entity can choose to present this information as part of its Statement of Activities, in the footnotes to the financial statements, or as a separate basic financial statement. Under ASU 2016-14, this required information cannot be presented in a supplemental schedule. Larger, more complex organizations may choose to present this analysis in a separate statement rather than try to include this in the Statement of Activities because of the volume of information if there are multiple programs and supporting services.

As part of the ASU 2016-14 implementation process, entities should evaluate their current classification of major programs and supporting services. They should examine whether there are activities that should be combined into one program or supporting service to streamline the presentation of activities in the financial statements.

In addition to the analysis of expenses, the ASU requires that entities disclose their expense allocation methodology in the footnotes. The adoption of the new ASU is a good time for entities to reexamine their cost-allocation methodologies.

Steps to Analyze the Statement of Functional Expenses

Use the Statement of Functional Expenses to analyze the categories of expenses incurred by the organization. This analysis will show the significant expenses incurred for all programs and supporting services and allows you to see how resources are being deployed. When this statement is presented on a comparative basis, it can be used to analyze the components of significant expenses from one year to the next.

CHAPTER 11

Footnotes to Financial Statements

Footnotes play a major role in helping you understand an organization's financial situation. The footnotes begin by highlighting significant accounting policies and then go on to detail matters of significance. Major acquisitions, or changes in operations, are highlighted, as are pension requirements, pending lawsuits, and other significant information. Some financial statements may contain footnotes that are unique to nonprofit organizations. These include footnotes related to contributions receivable, pledges receivable, investments, restricted support and net assets, and joint fundraising costs that provide valuable information about the organization's operations.

Whenever you read a financial statement that contains footnotes, be sure to read the footnotes. A general rule of thumb, you should spend at least as much time reading the footnotes as you do reading the financial statements. The footnotes are the road map to the financial statements and provide the story behind the numbers. The footnotes contain the information that explains many of the significant and material numbers presented in the financial statements and are critical to understanding an organization. The footnotes will often provide the detail for amounts presented at an aggregated level in the face of the financial statements.

Audited financial statements present the accounting policies of the nonprofit organization as the first section of the footnotes. These footnotes will provide the reader with an understanding of the accounting policies being followed by the entity for its assets, liabilities, net assets, revenue, and expenses. Following the accounting policies are other footnotes that support the items presented in the financial statements.

The determination as to what information is included in the footnotes is governed by technical guidance issued by the FASB. Some of the key footnotes that readers should focus on include related-party transactions, contingencies, and subsequent events. If the auditor's report also includes an Other Matters or an Emphasis of a Matter section, readers should refer to the footnote(s) referenced to understand the consequences of these items on the financial statements.

There are several new and enhanced disclosure requirements required once the entity adopts ASU 2016-14. The purpose of these new disclosures is to provide more information and greater transparency in the financial statements, thus making it more important than ever to focus attention on the footnotes.

General highlights of new and enhanced disclosures under ASU 2016-14 include:

a. Amounts and purposes of governing board designations, appropriations, and similar actions that result in self-imposed limits on the use of resources without donor-imposed restrictions as of the end of the reporting period.

b. Composition of net assets with donor restrictions at the end of the reporting period and how the restrictions affect the use of resources.

c. Qualitative information that communicates how a nonprofit manages its liquid resources available to meet cash needs for general expenditures within one year after the Statement of Financial Position (Balance Sheet) date.

d. Quantitative information, either on the face of the Statement of Financial Position (Balance Sheet) or in the footnotes, and additional qualitative information in the footnotes, as necessary, that communicates the availability of a nonprofit's financial assets at the Statement of Financial Position date to meet cash needs for general expenditures within one year after the Statement of Financial Position date. Availability of a financial asset may be affected by:

   1. Its nature.
   2. External limits imposed by donors, grantors, laws, and contracts with others.
   3. Internal limits imposed by governing board decisions.

e. Amounts of expenses by both their natural classification and their functional classification. This analysis of expenses is to be provided in one location, which could be on the face of the Statement of Activities, as a separate statement, or in the footnotes to the financial statements.

f. Method(s) used to allocate costs among program and supporting functions.

g. Underwater endowment funds, which include required disclosures of:

   1. A nonprofit's policy, and any actions taken during the period concerning appropriation from underwater endowment funds.
   2. The aggregate fair value of such funds.
   3. The aggregate of the original gift amounts (or level required by the donor or law) to be maintained.
   4. The aggregate amount by which funds are underwater (deficiencies), which are to be classified as part of net assets with donor restrictions.

CHAPTER 12

Internal versus External (Audited) Financial Statements

Organization Management Statements

Most financial statements are created internally by the nonprofit's management to use as management tools and reporting mechanisms to the organization's board. These statements usually include a Statement of Financial Position and a Statement of Activities for the organization as a whole. Occasionally, they will also include a Statement of Cash Flows and, more rarely still, footnotes. Such internal financial statements frequently include detailed Statements of Activities for each department, and sometimes for units within departments. These statements are essential for management of the organization. They are often used in conjunction with determining where an organization stands related to its board-approved budget. Internal financial statements should be produced on a regular and timely basis so that the organization's managers can identify issues promptly after the end of the accounting period and respond accordingly. The entity will oftentimes provide internal statements to various committees of the board throughout the year as well as to outside creditors or grantors.

Audited Financial Statements

At year-end, many nonprofits have their financial statements audited by independent certified public accountants (CPAs), who state whether the financial statements present fairly in all material respects the financial position of the organization and its activities and cash flows for the period in question. These audited financial statements are required to provide all the basic financial statements, at a minimum, and a complete set of footnotes. The audited financial statements are required to be prepared in accordance with accounting principles generally accepted in the United States of America (U.S. GAAP) as promulgated by the Financial Accounting Standards Board (FASB). In some instances, an organization may choose another basis of accounting. If this occurs, the entity is required to discuss the alternative basis in the footnotes and the reasons for their departure from GAAP. The key item of value in these audited financial statements is not just the figures, but that an independent third party is attesting to their reasonableness in his or her report.

CHAPTER 13

The Independent Auditor's Report

The independent auditor's report states his or her opinion regarding the audited financial statements. It is the culmination of a thorough examination of each of the financial statements and the data underlying them. An *unmodified* (clean) opinion is issued when the auditor is satisfied with the financial statements as a whole and they are presented in accordance with U.S. GAAP.

What It Does (and Does Not) Mean to Be "Clean"

A clean opinion provides the highest level of assurance that in all "material" (significant) respects (1) the Statement of Financial Position fairly presents the organization's financial position; (2) the Statement of Activities fairly presents the results of the organization's operations; and (3) the Statement of Cash Flows fairly presents its cash flows. The reader of these statements can be confident that appropriate accounting principles have been followed and that appropriate accounting principles have been used consistently to maintain comparability of financial statements from period to period. The reader can also be confident that any significant matters not shown on the face of the financial statements are adequately disclosed in the footnotes.

However, the reader should not look to the audited financial statements for perfect accuracy. Based on auditing standards generally accepted in the United States of America (GAAS), when conducting an audit of financial statements, the auditor must obtain reasonable assurance about whether the audited financial statements are free from material misstatement. Based on GAAS, reasonable assurance is a high, but not absolute, level of assurance. The independent auditor's report also does not comment on immaterial matters, and audited financial statements are frequently the end result of many judgment calls regarding what is material (significant) and what is not.

The independent auditor's report does not deliver an opinion on the organization's financial condition. To the extent that the audited financial statements *present fairly* the organization's financial condition, however, the reader obtains sufficient information for forming such an opinion. Another caveat about the independent auditor's opinion is that it *does not* discuss the competence, skills, or knowledge of the organization's management. You must look elsewhere to obtain that information. Oftentimes external auditors will prepare a management letter that may discuss such issues that were noted during the audit of the organization.

If the auditor has concerns about whether the entity can continue operations that cannot be alleviated by looking at future operations or other pertinent information, he or she may add an Emphasis of a Matter paragraph that discusses the fact that he or she is concerned with the ability of the entity to continue operations. If this is necessary, the auditor will include an additional paragraph that discusses this issue and draws the reader's attention to a specific footnote that will contain additional information. This scenario can become more common in negative economic climates.

A Clean Opinion Always Contains the Same Information

Financial statement readers rely heavily on an auditor's opinion. CPAs almost always use the same language and format to express an unmodified opinion so that this type of opinion can be readily identified. *Every time you read an audited financial statement, look for the following information in the independent auditor's report.*

Sample Unmodified Independent Auditor's Report on the Financial Statements

We have audited the accompanying financial statements of (Name of Nonprofit), which comprise the statement of financial position as of December 31, 20XX, and the related statements of activities and cash flows for the year then ended, and the related notes to the financial statements.

Management's Responsibility for the Financial Statements

Management is responsible for the preparation and fair presentation of these financial statements in accordance with accounting principles generally accepted in the United States of America; this includes the design, implementation, and maintenance of internal control relevant to the preparation and fair presentation of financial statements that are free from material misstatement, whether due to fraud or error.

Auditor's Responsibility

Our responsibility is to express an opinion on these financial statements based on our audit. We conducted our audit in accordance with auditing standards generally accepted in the United States of America. Those standards require that we plan and perform the audit to obtain reasonable assurance about whether the financial statements are free from material misstatement.

An audit involves performing procedures to obtain audit evidence about the amounts and disclosures in the financial statements. The procedures selected depend on the auditor's judgment, including the assessment of the risks of material misstatement of the financial statements, whether due to fraud or error. In making those risk assessments, the auditor considers internal control relevant to the entity's preparation and fair presentation of the financial statements in order to design audit procedures that are appropriate in the circumstances, but not for the purpose of expressing an opinion on the effectiveness of the entity's internal control. Accordingly, we express no such opinion. An audit also includes evaluating the appropriateness of accounting policies used and the reasonableness of significant accounting estimates made by management, as well as evaluating the overall presentation of the financial statements.

We believe that the audit evidence we have obtained is sufficient and appropriate to provide a basis for our audit opinion.

Opinion

In our opinion, the financial statements referred to above present fairly, in all material respects, the financial position of (Name of Nonprofit) as of December 31, 20XX, and the changes in its net assets and its cash flows for the year then ended in accordance with accounting principles generally accepted in the United States of America.

The first paragraph of the independent auditor's report tells you the names and dates or time periods of the audited financial statements. This first paragraph will include all financial statements audited and the periods covered. The second paragraph explains management's responsibility for the financial statements. The third through fifth paragraphs explain the independent auditor's responsibility and the nature of audit procedures and that the auditors have performed their work according to established professional guidelines. The sixth paragraph, the *opinion paragraph,* states the auditor's opinion that the financial statements are "present[ed] fairly, in all material respects . . . [and] in accordance with accounting principles generally accepted in the United States of America."

When these paragraphs are present, you can be confident that the independent auditor's report is clean and rely on the financial statements accordingly. An unmodified opinion sometimes includes an additional paragraph that draws the reader's attention to a particular matter. This additional paragraph does not reduce the level of assurance the independent auditor is expressing. It simply provides disclosure of additional information in the audited financial statements, or an additional important matter. For example, a seventh or eighth paragraph might indicate that the information is presented in a different fashion from in the previous year or discuss an unusual or important subsequent event.

These additional paragraphs are referred to as either an "Emphasis of a Matter" or "Other Matter" paragraph and will be labeled as such in the independent auditor's report. An *Emphasis of a Matter* paragraph is included in the independent auditor's report to refer to a matter appropriately presented or disclosed in the audited financial statements that is relevant to the users' understanding of the financial statements. Some common examples of topics addressed in an *Emphasis of a Matter* paragraph include when an auditor reports on an incomplete presentation but one that is otherwise in accordance with GAAP (that is, an entity presents the statement of activities by type of net asset in a columnar format for the current year but only presents a total column for the prior year), a change in accounting principle, or a correction of a misstatement.

An *other matter* paragraph is included in the independent auditor's report and refers to a matter other than those appropriately presented and disclosed in the audited financial statements that is relevant to the users' understanding of the audit, the auditor's responsibility, or the auditor's report. Some common examples of topics addressed in an *other matter* paragraph include the independent auditor's report on supplemental information accompanying the audited financial statements and prior period financial statements not being audited.

CHAPTER 14

Other Types of Auditor Opinions

An unmodified opinion provides the highest level of assurance that an audit can provide. Other types of opinions are possible, and there are varying degrees of assurance associated with them. A *modified* opinion occurs when the audited financial statements contain an issue that the CPA has reservations about, such as a departure from U.S. GAAP, or a limitation on the scope of the audit. An example of a departure from U.S. GAAP is where an organization chooses to not recognize a material amount of certain contributed services. An example of a scope limitation might occur if the external auditor is not able to observe and count year-end inventory because this has already occurred prior to their being engaged for the audit.

An *adverse* opinion presents a more serious problem. It occurs when financial statements are misleading and management will not correct them. Such financial statements may involve serious departures from U.S. GAAP and cannot be relied on to present fairly the financial position and the results of operations. A *disclaimer* of opinion occurs when the auditor is unable to form an opinion. A disclaimer must be issued when the auditor lacks independence or is unable to gather enough information to form an opinion (that is, the organization has incomplete records or records that cannot be audited).

These types of audit opinions can be identified by the language in the report that will include a paragraph that indicates the basis for the opinion and includes the applicable name of the report as listed at its top. It should be very clear from the report as to the type of opinion that the auditor issued.

CHAPTER 15

Supplemental Information

An organization being audited will frequently want to provide more detailed information than is required to be presented by U.S. GAAP. This additional information is considered supplemental information, or supplementary information, and is presented at the option of the organization. Some examples of supplemental information include consolidating financial schedules that provide information to support consolidated financial statements, details of certain expense categories, and other information the organization may feel will benefit readers of its financial statements.

The supplemental information always follows the footnotes. In these situations, the auditors will either include their opinion on the supplemental information in an additional paragraph to the auditor's report on the financial statements or include a separate opinion on the supplemental information only following the notes to the financial statements. This opinion, referred to as the Auditor's Opinion on Supplemental Information, will indicate the level of assurance the auditor is providing on the supplemental schedules.

Be advised that the level of assurance on the supplemental information is not at the same level as for the basic audited statements. The auditor's opinion on the supplemental information usually states either (1) the procedures applied during the financial statement audit were applied to the supplemental information and that the supplemental information is fairly stated in all material respects in relation to the financial statements as a whole; or (2) procedures applied during the audit were not applied to the supplemental information and therefore the supplemental information presented is marked "unaudited."

CHAPTER 16

Reserves

There are many arguments for having nonprofits establish an operating reserve since many activities that they engage in expose them to financial burdens. As an example, government contracts often require nonprofits to hire staff and deliver services for 30 to 60 days before receiving any reimbursement. Government and private funding sources may reduce or delay grants with very little warning, often putting nonprofits at great risk. At times major fundraising events may get delayed or canceled. These are only a few examples of circumstances where an operating reserve would be needed.

With so much uncertainty associated with a nonprofit's varied sources of income, operating reserves are essential to giving nonprofits and their board's breathing room and the ability to respond to the rapidly changing environment in which we now live and work in without lurching from one financial crisis to the next.

However, operating reserves are more than just a safety net for catastrophic circumstances and the unexpected. They also provide nonprofits a chance to be able to respond to unanticipated opportunities, such as the expansion of an existing program, development of new programs, purchase of property, or even acquisition and merger of another nonprofit.

A common question often asked by CEOs and their boards is, "What is an appropriate level of reserves for our organization?"

The answer: it is best to start by saying that based on the literature available, there is simply no single correct solution for all organizations. Despite the importance of the issue, there is no agreed-upon industry benchmark. Part of the problem is that to have benchmarks that apply to all nonprofits is difficult because of the wide array of business models used by nonprofits. To complicate matters further, such benchmarks as are commonly used must be viewed in the context of the particular entity to which they are being applied.

The problems: there is actually a variety of problems in trying to establish an industry standard benchmark. Two of the more common issues encountered relate to:

1. The most important is that the term *reserve*, while generally understood, is subject to a great variety of specific definitions.
2. A close second in solving the problem is the variety of the potential contextual issues in which the association finds itself. This is where we will begin.

Contextual Issues

The initial contextual issue concerns the age of the organization. Simply put, a young organization will not have had time to build a significant reserve. These organizations should have as their goal to create a positive change in net assets every year so they can build a reserve. Such a goal should not be less than 3 to 5 percent of gross income and not more than 8 to 10 percent. While these numbers are not written in stone, they are logic-driven: to take less will not allow the organization to aggregate a sufficient reserve, or perhaps even keep up with inflation. To take more would deprive the young organization from offering sufficient programs for its members or those it provides services to.

One of the most important contextual issues concerns the number and dependability of the organization's income streams. If an organization has three or more major revenue streams that are reasonably dependable, they are far more secure and thus need less money to be available for a rainy day (that is, reserves). On the other hand, an organization that has few or no highly reliable income streams might do quite well to have nine months' or a year's worth of expenses in reserve.

Some organizations also need to maintain more reserves than others because of major planned expenditures such as the purchase of a building, expansion of program activities, or a major information technology implementation. While borrowing is used as frequently as cash for expenditures of this type of activity, it is nevertheless important for an organization when setting its current goals for reserves to do so with an eye toward potential major expenditures or programmatic expansion.

The fourth contextual issue is based on whether the organization is likely to confront "difficult to anticipate" contingencies. For example, large rescue organizations must have very substantial reserves since they may face some years in which there are a multitude of devastating storms, whereas a professional society is not likely to face similar contingencies.

The final contextual issue is one of absolute size. If an organization has one or two million dollars a year in expenditures, having three to six months' worth of expenditures in reserves may make good sense. On the other hand, if an organization has a $50 million budget, it might well be considered poor stewardship to have a substantial percentage of that in reserve. Members or stakeholders may question why so large a sum of money is being held by the organization while they are still being asked to pay an increased amount of dues or make contributions to the organization.

Common Calculations of Reserves

The variety of calculations of reserves used within the nonprofit industry is broad indeed. Among the many definitions organizations use for reserves are:

1. Total assets
2. Total assets less total liabilities (or net assets)

3. Current assets plus investments minus current liabilities
4. Or simply total cash and investments

Some organizations fund their reserves with "liquid reserves," which they define as "cash and investments that can be quickly converted to cash." The problem with this definition is that it does not take into account such things as accounts payable and deferred revenue, and the like, which will be paid or consumed in the very near term. Nevertheless, it is a commonly used definition.

Other organizations use "total net assets." The problem with this figure, which is self-defining, is that it would include fixed assets such as a building, computers, or furniture and fixtures—all of which are not available to be spent should the need arise. This method also doesn't exclude restricted net assets. On the other hand, total net assets would have been potentially reduced by long-term liabilities, such as mortgages, which do not need to be paid off and thus do not require the use of cash any time soon.

An alternative reserve calculation has been developed by The Nonprofit Operating Reserves Initiative Workgroup. This is an all-volunteer group of nonprofit leaders, financial-management consultants, and others sponsored by the National Center for Charitable Statistics, Center on Nonprofits and Philanthropy at the Urban Institute, and United Way Worldwide. This group recognized the problem with trying to calculate reserves and has produced a white paper and a toolkit to help nonprofits and their boards better understand what reserves are and why they need them.

A More Precise and Conservative Definition of Reserves

Arguably, the best measure of what a nonprofit organization has available to use in case of an urgent need for liquidity is based on the elements that define liquidity. Consider the following very strict formula for *available reserves.*

Financial Assets

LESS These Assets:
• Receivables that are not fully expected to be collected within three months
• Inventory that is not fully expected to be sold for cash within three months
• Prepaid expenses and other assets
• Restricted investments or other liquid assets included in financial assets

LESS These Liabilities:
• Current liabilities, except for deferred revenue

This formula essentially reduces the financial position of the organization to its ultimate measure of available liquidity. Begin with all financial assets, but take out accounts receivable, inventory, prepaid expenses, and funds that are restricted by donor stipulation or designated by the board for other uses which may or may not be converted to cash in the very short term. Then add in the investments that the organization could spend if it had to. Finally, subtract out all the current liabilities except for amounts collected in advance of providing goods or services. What remains is an ultimate measure of liquidity and thus funds available to meet any emergency. This calculation is very similar to the new liquidity analysis required under ASU 2016-14; however, these are not meant to be the same.

The formula is quite conservative. This still does not directly answer the question of the actual reserve size, however. Unfortunately, there is no answer that works for all organizations all the time. Each organization has to make its own determination based on its circumstances. An often quoted rule of thumb is that a desirable reserve level should be somewhere between three and six months' worth of expenditures.

Once an organization decides on the desired reserve size, there are several different ways the actual reserve can be handled. Some organizations simply monitor their unrestricted net assets to ensure these exceed the reserve level. Other organizations like to place their reserve funds in a separate bank or investment account to segregate these funds. Some organizations pass board resolutions that establish the reserve as board-designated net assets and show these on the Statement of Financial Position. ASU 2016-14 requires that organizations disclose all board-designated net assets either on the face of the Statement of Financial Position or in the footnotes.

You will see in the exercises in the book that Examples 3A and 3B present an entity that shows reserves.

CHAPTER 17

Financial Statement Exercises

The three sets of financial statements provided are illustrative financial statements developed to be representative of actual nonprofit organizations' financial statements. To provide you with the greatest educational opportunity, the nature and condition of each organization varies in substantial ways from the others.

Each set of examples has two distinct presentations shown. The first example in each set is labeled as "A" and is prepared using current accounting guidance prior to adoption of ASU 2016-14. The second example in each set is labeled as "B" and is prepared after the adoption of ASU 2016-14.

- The first set of examples, the Society of American Associations, is a reasonably large trade association that has challenges, but is at a mature point in its existence.
- The second set of examples, The United States Charity, has only been in existence for approximately a year and a half. It too faces interesting challenges.
- The third and final set of examples is the Society of Analysts, which presents the consolidated financial statements of an association and its foundation. What makes this statement particularly interesting is that only one year's financial information is being provided. Despite the lack of comparative information, a great deal of insight can still be gained.

The first example statement in each set is followed by a series of questions that will help you increase your expertise in working with such financial statements. These questions are of the type that a beginning reader of financial statements should be able to answer. They do not concern the most technical aspects of the financial statements that are often discussed in the footnotes. The last question regarding each financial statement is to identify the most important issues revealed by the financial statements. It is this type of insight that is the key goal of every financial statement reader.

The second example statement in each set is followed by a series of questions that are designed to highlight and focus on the new information required by ASU 2016-14 in addition to the questions designed to increase your expertise in working with nonprofit financial statements.

CHAPTER 18

Example Set 1

The following examples refer to a trade association, the Society of American Associations. The examples present the comparative financial statements for the years that ended December 31, 2016 and 2015.

Example 1A: Prepared using accounting guidance before the adoption of ASU 2016-14.

Example 1B: Prepared after the adoption of ASU 2016-14.

Example 1A

Society of American Associations

Before the Adoption of ASU 2016-14

Financial Statements

Years Ended December 31, 2016 and 2015

Example 1A

Society of American Associations

Independent Auditor's Report

To the Board of Directors of
Society of American Associations

Report on the Financial Statements

We have audited the accompanying statements of the **Society of American Associations** (the Society), which comprise the statements of financial position as of December 31, 2016 and 2015, and the related statements of activities and cash flows for the years then ended, and the related notes to the financial statements.

Management's Responsibility for the Financial Statements

Management is responsible for the preparation and fair presentation of these financial statements in accordance with accounting principles generally accepted in the United States of America; this includes the design, implementation, and maintenance of internal control relevant to the preparation and fair presentation of financial statements that are free from material misstatement, whether due to fraud or error.

Auditor's Responsibility

Our responsibility is to express an opinion on these financial statements based on our audits. We conducted our audits in accordance with auditing standards generally accepted in the United States of America. Those standards require that we plan and perform the audit to obtain reasonable assurance about whether the financial statements are free from material misstatement.

An audit involves performing procedures to obtain audit evidence about the amounts and disclosures in the financial statements. The procedures selected depend on the auditor's judgment, including the assessment of the risks of material misstatement of the financial statements, whether due to fraud or error. In making those risk assessments, the auditor considers internal control relevant to the entity's preparation and fair presentation of the financial statements in order to design audit procedures that are appropriate in the circumstances, but not for the purpose of expressing an opinion on the effectiveness of the entity's internal control. Accordingly, we express no such opinion. An audit also includes evaluating the appropriateness of accounting policies used and the reasonableness of significant accounting estimates made by management, as well as evaluating the overall presentation of the financial statements.

We believe that the audit evidence we have obtained is sufficient and appropriate to provide a basis for our audit opinion.

Example 1A

Society of American Associations

Opinion

In our opinion, the financial statements referred to above present fairly, in all material respects, the financial position of the **Society of American Associations** as of December 31, 2016 and 2015, and the changes in its net assets and its cash flows for the years then ended, in accordance with accounting principles generally accepted in the United States of America.

February 14, 2017

Example 1A

Entity uses a classified presentation which shows current and noncurrent assets and liabilities.

Society of American Associations

Statements of Financial Position

December 31,	2016	2015
Assets		
Current assets		
Cash and cash equivalents	$ 31,830,448	$ 30,351,846
Accounts receivable—net of allowance		
for uncollectible accounts of $23,829		
in 2016 and 2015	1,448,668	7,694,031
Prepaid expenses—annual meeting	16,288,599	16,702,264
Prepaid expenses and other assets	823,352	680,338
Total current assets	50,391,067	55,428,479
Noncurrent assets		
Long-term investments	44,849,774	56,534,947
Property and equipment, net	44,863,787	45,186,925
Prepaid expenses—annual meeting—net of current portion	106,900	363,945
Total noncurrent assets	89,820,461	102,085,817
Total assets	$ 140,211,528	$ 157,514,296
Liabilities and Net Assets		
Current liabilities		
Accounts payable	$ 4,770,576	$ 5,528,746
Accrued expenses	4,756,708	3,272,547
Deferred revenue	61,505,829	65,655,307
Total current liabilities	71,033,113	74,456,600
Commitments and contingencies		
Unrestricted net assets	69,178,415	83,057,696
Total liabilities and net assets	$ 140,211,528	$ 157,514,296

Entity only has unrestricted net assets.

See accompanying summary of accounting policies and notes to financial statements.

Shaded lines indicate the basic totals that must be presented.

Example 1A

Society of American Associations

Statements of Activities

Years ended December 31,	2016	2015
Revenues		
Annual meeting	$ 68,083,991	$ 78,701,680
Membership dues	3,791,142	3,760,127
Meetings and conferences	2,194,980	2,065,282
Fees and assessments	1,008,227	1,061,717
Publication sales	826,890	1,078,996
Other income	62,185	42,149
Total revenues	75,967,415	86,709,951
Expenses		
Program services		
Annual meeting	38,937,135	35,737,453
Communications	8,591,621	8,274,453
Government and legal affairs	6,069,584	5,370,725
Member relations and customer service	5,244,459	5,458,744
Meetings and conferences	4,209,099	4,170,591
Technology and standards	3,122,172	3,014,999
Market research	2,807,570	3,105,830
Total program services	68,981,640	65,132,795
Supporting services		
General and administrative	7,502,154	8,141,724
Total expenses	76,483,794	73,274,519
(Decrease) increase in unrestricted net assets from operations	(516,379)	13,435,432
Nonoperating activities		
Net investment (loss)/gain	(13,362,902)	2,884,198
Change in net assets	(13,879,281)	16,319,630
Unrestricted net assets, beginning of year	83,057,696	66,738,066
Unrestricted net assets, end of year	$ 69,178,415	$ 83,057,696

> Entity chose to show nonoperating items.

See accompanying summary of accounting policies and notes to financial statements.

Example 1A

Society of American Associations

Statements of Cash Flows

Years ended December 31,	2016	2015
Cash flows from operating activities		
Change in net assets	$ (13,879,281)	$ 16,319,630
Adjustments to reconcile change in net assets to		
net cash provided by operating activities:		
Depreciation and amortization	1,570,340	1,060,589
Net realized and unrealized losses on investments	15,413,595	204,131
Bad debts	–	14
(Increase) decrease in assets		
Accounts receivable	6,245,363	(5,840,015)
Prepaid expenses—annual meeting	670,710	(1,376,880)
Prepaid expenses and other assets	(143,014)	(111,725)
Increase (decrease) in liabilities		
Accounts payable	(758,170)	1,245,865
Accrued expenses	1,484,161	694,444
Deferred revenue	(4,149,478)	361,487
Net cash provided by operating activities	6,454,226	12,557,540
Cash flows from investing activities		
Proceeds from sale of investments	70,439,883	22,064,663
Purchases of investments	(74,168,305)	(30,839,230)
Proceeds from sales of property and equipment	53,800	–
Purchases of property and equipment	(1,301,002)	(6,194,088)
Net cash used in investing activities	(4,975,624)	(14,968,655)
Increase (decrease) in cash and cash equivalents	1,478,602	(2,411,115)
Cash and cash equivalents, beginning of year	30,351,846	32,762,961
Cash and cash equivalents, end of year	$ 31,830,448	$ 30,351,846

See accompanying summary of accounting policies and notes to financial statements.

Example 1A

Society of American Associations

Notes to Financial Statements

Summary of Accounting Policies:

Society

The Society of American Associations (the Society) is a tax-exempt trade association dedicated to the business interests of associations that operate in the United States. The majority of its revenue is derived from the annual meeting.

Basis of Accounting

The financial statements of the Society are presented in conformity with accounting principles generally accepted in the United States of America (U.S. GAAP) and have been prepared on the accrual basis of accounting.

Cash and Cash Equivalents

Cash and cash equivalents consist of highly liquid investments with original maturity dates of three months or less, excluding money market accounts held as part of long-term investments. The Society maintains cash balances which may exceed federally insured limits. The Society does not believe that this results in any significant credit risk.

Accounts Receivable

Accounts receivable consists primarily of amounts due from the sale of publications, advertising and annual meeting registrations. The allowance method is used to determine the uncollectible amounts. The allowance is based upon prior years' experience and management's analysis of subsequent collections.

Allowances on accounts receivable are recorded when circumstances indicate collection is doubtful for particular accounts receivable or as a general reserve for all accounts receivable. Accounts receivable are written off if reasonable collection efforts prove unsuccessful. Bad debt expense is included in general and administrative expense in the statements of activities when allowances on accounts receivable are increased or when accounts written off exceed available allowances.

Prepaid Expenses: Annual Meeting

Prepaid expenses consist primarily of payments made by the Society to vendors in conjunction with the annual meeting which is held in May of each year. These payments are recognized as expenses in the year of the annual meeting.

Example 1A

Society of American Associations

Notes to Financial Statements

Long-term Investments

Investments in mutual funds are valued at fair value, based upon the net asset value per share as determined by quoted market prices. The preferred stock is valued based on market quotations from similar companies. The Society's investment in the venture capital fund has no readily determined market value and is valued at the net asset value per share practical expedient. Because of the inherent uncertainty of valuation, it is reasonably possible that such estimated values may differ significantly from the values that would have been used had a ready market for the securities existed, and the differences could be material.

Unrealized and realized gains and losses on investments are included in the accompanying statements of activities as nonoperating activity.

Property and Equipment

Property and equipment are stated at cost. The Society capitalizes all expenditures for property and equipment over $5,000. Depreciation and amortization are computed using the straight-line method over the estimated useful lives of the assets or the lesser of the minimum lease period or the asset's useful life for leasehold improvements. When assets are sold or otherwise disposed of, the asset and related accumulated depreciation and amortization are removed from the accounts, and any remaining gain or loss is included in operations. Repairs and maintenance are charged to expense when incurred.

Certain costs of internally developed software and website development are capitalized. The costs are being amortized over the estimated useful lives of the software and website.

Impairment of Long-Lived Assets

Management of the Society reviews asset carrying amounts whenever events or circumstances indicate that such carrying amounts may not be recoverable. When considered impaired, the carrying amount of the asset is reduced, by a charge in the statements of activities, to its current fair value.

Deferred Revenue

The Society defers amounts received in advance for the annual meeting and other meetings and conferences to be held in subsequent years. These receipts are recognized as income in the year the related meeting is held . Amounts received in 2016 and 2015 relating to deposits from exhibitors for the annual meeting to be conducted in 2017 and 2016 were $60,543,643 and $64,800,745, respectively. Amounts received for future annual meetings are included in deferred revenue in the accompanying statements of financial position.

Example 1A

Society of American Associations

Notes to Financial Statements

Unrestricted Net Assets

Unrestricted net assets are available for use in general operations.

Revenue Recognition

The annual meeting and other meetings and conferences revenue is recognized as revenue in the year the meeting or conference is held. Membership dues are recognized as revenue ratably over the calendar year membership term. Fees and assessments are recognized as revenue when the amounts are earned. Publication sales revenue is recognized at the time of sale.

Expenses

Expenses are recognized by the Society on an accrual basis. Expenses paid in advance and not yet incurred are recorded as prepaid until the applicable period.

Measure of Operations

For purposes of this presentation, the Society considers net investment return to be nonoperating.

Liquidity and Availability

Entity chose to present this information prior to adoption of ASU 2016-14.

The Society manages its liquid resources by focusing on investing excess cash in investments that maximize earnings potential balanced with the amount of risk the Society's Investment Committee has decided can be tolerated. The Society's investment policy is designed to ensure adequate financial assets are available to meet general expenditures, liabilities, and other obligations as they become due. The Society maintains easily liquidated investments in the long-term portfolio to meet its financial obligations. The Society focuses on collecting receivables timely to maximize the cash collections due to the Society. In addition, in order to manage the annual meeting each year the Society must make payments in advance to the meeting facility and vendors. The Society times these payments to maximize the time they have access to the cash.

The Society's financial assets available within one year of the statement of financial position date for general expenditure are as follows:

As of December 31, 2016,	
Cash and cash equivalents	$ 31,830,448
Accounts receivable	1,448,668
Subtotal	33,279,116
Money market and mutual funds held in long-term portfolio	35,891,011
	$ 69,170,127

Example 1A

Society of American Associations

Notes to Financial Statements

Functional Allocation of Expenses

The costs of providing various program and supporting activities have been summarized on a functional basis in the statements of activities. Accordingly, certain costs have been allocated among the programs and supporting services benefited.

Financial Instruments

Financial instruments which potentially subject the Society to concentrations of credit risk consist principally of cash and cash equivalents and investments held at creditworthy financial institutions. At times the Society's operating cash accounts exceed the federally insured limit. The credit risk with respect to accounts receivable is limited because the Society deals with a large number of members and customers in a wide geographic area.

Use of Estimates

The preparation of financial statements in conformity with accounting principles generally accepted in the United States of America requires management to make estimates and assumptions that affect the reported amounts of assets and liabilities, disclosure of contingent assets and liabilities at the date of the financial statements, and the reported amounts of revenues and expenses during the reporting period. Actual results could differ from those estimates.

Advertising Costs

The Society expenses advertising costs as incurred. For the years ended December 31, 2016 and 2015, the Society expensed advertising costs of $5,573,779 and $4,837,601, respectively.

Recent Accounting Pronouncement Adopted

In May 2015, the Financial Accounting Standards Board (FASB) issued Accounting Standards Update (ASU) 2015-07, "Disclosure for Investments in Certain Entities that Calculate Net Asset Value per Share," which eliminates the requirement to categorize investments in the fair value hierarchy if their fair value is measured at net asset value per share (or its equivalent). ASU 2015-07 is effective for fiscal years beginning after December 15, 2016 with early adoption permitted. The Society chose to adopt the provisions of ASU 2015-07 early and the updated disclosures are reflected in these statements. Other than the changes in the disclosures outlined above, there was no effect on the Society's financial statements as a result of adoption.

Recent Accounting Pronouncements to be Adopted

In May 2014, the FASB issued ASU 2014-09, "Revenue from Contracts with Customers (Topic 606)," which is a comprehensive new revenue recognition standard that will supersede existing revenue recognition guidance. The core principle of the guidance is that an entity should recognize revenue to depict the transfer of promised goods or services to customers in an amount that reflects the consideration to which the entity expects to be entitled in exchange for those goods or services. FASB issued ASU 2015-14 that deferred the effective date

Example 1A

Society of American Associations

Notes to Financial Statements

until annual periods beginning after December 15, 2018. Earlier adoption is permitted subject to certain limitations. The amendments in this update are required to be applied retrospectively to each prior reporting period presented or with the cumulative effect being recognized at the date of initial application. Management is currently evaluating the impact of this ASU on its financial statements.

In February 2016, the FASB issued ASU 2016-02, "Leases (Topic 842)," to increase transparency and comparability among organizations by recognizing lease assets and lease liabilities on the statement of financial position and disclosing key information about leasing arrangements for lessees and lessors. The new standard applies a right-of-use (ROU) model that requires, for all leases with a lease term of more than 12 months, an asset representing its right to use the underlying asset for the lease term and a liability to make lease payments to be recorded. The ASU is effective for fiscal years beginning after December 15, 2019 with early adoption permitted. Management is currently evaluating the impact of this ASU on its financial statements.

In August 2016, the FASB issued ASU 2016-14, "Not-for-Profit Entities (Topic 958): Presentation of Financial Statements of Not-for-Profit Entities." The ASU amends the current reporting model for nonprofit organizations and enhances their required disclosures. The major changes include: (a) requiring the presentation of only two classes of net assets now entitled "net assets without donor restrictions" and "net assets with donor restrictions," (b) modifying the presentation of underwater endowment funds and related disclosures, (c) requiring the use of the placed-in-service approach to recognize the expirations of restrictions on gifts used to acquire or construct long-lived assets absent explicit donor stipulations otherwise, (d) requiring that all nonprofits present an analysis of expenses by function and nature in either the statement of activities, a separate statement, or in the notes and disclose a summary of the allocation methods used to allocate costs, (e) requiring the disclosure of quantitative and qualitative information regarding liquidity and availability of resources, (f) presenting investment return net of external and direct internal investment expenses, and (g) modifying other financial statement reporting requirements and disclosures intended to increase the usefulness of nonprofit financial statements. The ASU is effective for the financial statements for fiscal years beginning after December 15, 2017. Early adoption is permitted. The provisions of the ASU must be applied on a retrospective basis for all years presented although certain optional practical expedients are available for periods prior to adoption. Management is currently evaluating the impact of this ASU on its financial statements.

Example 1A

Society of American Associations

Notes to Financial Statements

1. Tax Status

The Society has been granted exemption by the Internal Revenue Service (IRS) from Federal income taxes under Section 501(c)(6) of the Internal Revenue Code. However, income from certain activities not directly related to the Society's tax-exempt purpose is subject to taxation as unrelated income. The Society earns unrelated business income on advertising revenue. The Society reported no unrelated business income tax expense for the years ended December 31, 2016 and 2015.

Management believes it has no material uncertain tax positions or any related penalties and interest to accrue for the years ended December 31, 2016 and 2015. The Society is still open to examination by taxing authorities from year 2013 forward.

2. Fair Value Measurements

U.S. GAAP establishes a common definition for fair value to be applied under generally accepted accounting principles requiring use of fair value, establishes a framework for measuring fair value, and expands disclosures about such fair value measurements.

U.S. GAAP defines fair value as the price that would be received to sell an asset or paid to transfer a liability (i.e., the "exit price") in an orderly transaction between market participants at the measurement date. Measurement date is the date of the financial statements. U.S. GAAP establishes a hierarchy for inputs used in measuring fair value that maximizes the use of observable inputs and minimizes the use of unobservable inputs by requiring that observable inputs be used when available.

Observable inputs are inputs that market participants would use in pricing the asset or liability developed based on market data obtained from sources independent of the Society. Unobservable inputs are inputs that reflect the Society's estimates about the assumptions market participants would use in pricing the asset or liability developed based on the best information available under the circumstances.

The hierarchy is broken down into three levels based on the reliability of the inputs as follows:

Level 1: Valuation based on quoted market prices in active markets for identical assets or liabilities. Since valuations are based on quoted prices that are readily and regularly available in an active market, valuation of these products does not entail a significant degree of judgment.

Example 1A

Society of American Associations

Notes to Financial Statements

Level 2: Valuation based on quoted market prices of investments that are not actively traded or for which certain significant inputs are not observable, either directly or indirectly.

Level 3: Valuation based on inputs that are unobservable and significant to the overall fair value measurement.

The following is a description of the valuation methodologies used for assets measured at fair value. There have been no changes in the methodologies used at December 31, 2016 and 2015.

The money market funds, fixed income mutual funds, equity mutual funds, and balanced mutual funds are all valued at the net asset value of the fund as published at December 31, 2016 and 2015.

Preferred stock is valued using market quotations from similar companies to estimate the fair value.

The Society's alternative investment is a venture capital fund which is valued based on level 3 inputs within the investment hierarchy used in measuring fair value. Given the absence of market quotations, the fair value is estimated using the net asset value (NAV) per share provided to the Society by the investment firm. This NAV is used as a practical expedient. Individual holdings within the alternative investment may include investment in both nonmarketable and market-traded securities. Nonmarketable securities may include equity in private companies, real estate, thinly traded securities, and other investment vehicles. While the venture capital fund contains varying degrees of risk, the Society's exposure with respect to this investment is limited to its carrying amount (fair value as described above).

Example 1A

Society of American Associations

Notes to Financial Statements

The table below sets forth those assets measured at fair value as of December 31, 2016.

	Fair value measurement at reporting date using			
Description	Quoted prices in active markets for identical assets (level 1)	Significant other observable inputs (level 2)	Significant other unobservable inputs (level 3)	Balance as of December 31, 2016
Money market funds	$ 2,936,095	$ -	$ -	$ 2,936,095
Fixed income mutual funds	15,436,922	-	-	15,436,922
Equity mutual funds	15,209,336	-	-	15,209,336
Balanced mutual funds	2,308,658	-	-	2,308,658
Preferred stock	-	1,329,777	-	1,329,777
Total	$ 35,891,011	$ 1,329,777	$ -	37,220,788
Venture capital fund reported at net asset value*				7,628,986
Total				$ 44,849,774

* Certain investments that are measured at fair value using the net asset value per share (or its equivalent) practical expedient have not been categorized in the fair value hierarchy. The fair value amounts presented in this table are intended to permit reconciliation of the fair value hierarchy to the amounts presented in the accompanying statements of financial position.

Example 1A

Society of American Associations

Notes to Financial Statements

The table below sets forth those assets measured at fair value as of December 31, 2015.

| | Fair value measurement at reporting date using | | | |
Description	Quoted prices in active markets for identical assets (level 1)	Significant other observable inputs (level 2)	Significant other unobservable inputs (level 3)	Balance as of December 31, 2015
Money market funds	$ 225,282	$ -	$ -	$ 225,282
Fixed income mutual funds	13,775,000	-	-	13,775,000
Equity mutual funds	26,820,203	-	-	26,820,203
Balanced mutual funds	6,715,898	-	-	6,715,898
Preferred stock	-	599,999	-	599,999
Total	$ 47,536,383	$ 599,999	$ -	48,136,382
Venture capital fund reported at net asset value*				8,398,565
Total				$ 56,534,947

* Certain investments that are measured at fair value using the net asset value per share (or its equivalent) practical expedient have not been categorized in the fair value hierarchy. The fair value amounts presented in this table are intended to permit reconciliation of the fair value hierarchy to the amounts presented in the accompanying statements of financial position.

Example 1A

Society of American Associations

Notes to Financial Statements

The following table summarizes the change in the fair value for the Level 3 item for the years ended December 31, 2016 and 2015:

	Fair value measurement at reporting date using unobservable inputs (Level 3)
	Venture capital fund
Balance, January 1, 2015	$ 8,408,771
Total unrealized losses	(10,206)
Transfers (to) from other investments	-
Balance, December 31, 2015	8,398,565
Total unrealized losses	(769,579)
Transfers (to) from other investments	-
Balance, December 31, 2016	$ 7,628,986

The following table sets forth a summary of the Society's investment with a reported NAV for the year ended December 31, 2016.

Investment	Fair Value	Unfunded Commitments	Redemption Frequency	Notice Period
Venture Capital Fund	$ 7,628,986	$ -	Monthly	10 days

3. Investment Return

Investment (losses) gains consist of the following:

Years ended December 31,	2016	2015
Dividends and interest	$ 2,506,328	$ 3,634,504
Investment expenses	(455,635)	(546,175)
Unrealized losses on investments	(10,670,481)	(501,051)
Realized (losses) gains on investments	(4,743,114)	296,920
Total investment (losses) gains	$ (13,362,902)	$ 2,884,198

The Society already allocated direct internal investment expenses prior to adoption of ASU 2016-14.

Example 1A

Society of American Associations

Notes to Financial Statements

**4. Property and
    Equipment**

Property and equipment consists of the following at:

December 31,	2016	2015
Building and improvements	$ 38,597,469	$ 38,597,469
Computer software and hardware	2,158,515	3,750,184
Furniture and equipment	2,036,965	2,010,689
Telecommunications	748,851	748,851
Building improvements	5,807,311	4,876,329
	49,349,111	49,983,522
Less: accumulated depreciation and amortization	(4,485,324)	(4,796,597)
Total	$ 44,863,787	$ 45,186,925

Depreciation and amortization expense for the years ended December 31, 2016 and 2015 were $1,570,340 and $1,060,589, respectively.

Example 1A

Society of American Associations

Notes to Financial Statements

5. Commitments and Contingencies

Operating Leases

The Society has entered into certain noncancelable operating leases for equipment which expire on various dates through 2019. The following schedule reflects the future minimum lease payments under all operating lease agreements:

Years Ending December 31,		
2017	$	33,342
2018		33,342
2019		5,557
Total	$	72,241

Rent expense for the years ended December 31, 2016 and 2015 was $33,342.

Pending Litigation

The Society is subject to various legal proceedings and claims, including patent infringement and antitrust violations, in the ordinary course of its business affairs. The Society cannot reasonably estimate the outcomes of these proceedings, and the Society intends to continue to vigorously defend its position in these matters. In the opinion of management, the potential adverse impact of these legal proceedings and claims is insignificant to the financial statements of the Society.

Other

The Society is committed under agreements for annual meeting space for future years. The total commitment under the agreements is not determinable as it depends upon attendance and other unknown factors. In the event that the Society cancels the agreements, it has agreed to pay liquidating damages.

Example 1A

Society of American Associations

Notes to Financial Statements

6. **Benefit Plan**   *Employee 401(k) Plan*

The Society maintains, for the benefit of all its employees, a deferred compensation arrangement established under Section 401(k) of the Internal Revenue Code (IRC). Employees may defer a portion of their salary up to the maximum amount allowable under Section 415 of the IRC. In 2016 and 2015, the Society contributed 100% of a participant's first 6% of contributions. Participants are fully vested in all matching contributions. During 2016 and 2015, the Society's contributions to the 401(k) plan totaled $717,564 and $718,440, respectively.

7. **Subsequent Events**   The Society has evaluated subsequent events through February 14, 2017, which is the date the financial statements were available to be issued. There were no events that required adjustments to or disclosure in these financial statements.

Exercise 1A: Working with Financial Statements

Use the financial statements in Example 1A for the Society of American Associations to familiarize yourself with a basic nonprofit financial statement that presents full comparative information for two years.

1. Begin by looking at the independent auditor's report:
   a. What type of opinion is this?

      _____

      _____

   b. What period is covered by the report?

      _____

      _____

2. Locate the (1) Statements of Financial Position, (2) Statements of Activities, and (3) Statements of Cash Flows:
   a. How much are total current assets on December 31, 2016?

      _____

      _____

   b. How much are total noncurrent assets on December 31, 2016?

      _____

      _____

   c. How much are total liabilities on December 31, 2016?

      _____

      _____

   d. How much are total unrestricted net assets on December 31, 2016?

      _____

      _____

   e. What is the organization's change in net assets (bottom line) for the organization's year that ended on December 31, 2016 (FY 2016)?

      _____

      _____

3. Focusing on the Statements of Financial Position:
   a. Has the organization's current ratio (current assets/current liabilities) improved or declined from FY 2015 to FY 2016?

      _____

      _____

b. How much does the organization have in long-term investments on December 31, 2016?

_____

_____

c. How much are total prepaid expenses—annual meeting?

_____

_____

d. What is the allowance for uncollectible accounts receivable on December 31, 2016?

_____

_____

e. What is the organization's largest liability?

_____

_____

4. Moving to the Statements of Activities:
   a. How does the change in unrestricted net assets from operations for FY 2016 compare to those for FY 2015?

   _____

   _____

   b. What is the key source of revenue?

   _____

   _____

   c. What was the amount of the change in net assets from operations for the year that ended on December 31, 2016?

   _____

   _____

   d. What was the net investment return for FY 2016 versus FY 2015?

   _____

   _____

   e. What was the amount of the change in net assets for FY 2016 versus the amount of the change in net assets for FY 2015?

   _____

   _____

5. On to the Statements of Cash Flows:
   a. What method of presentation did the organization use for the statement?

   _____

   _____

b. What was the amount of cash and cash equivalents provided by or used in operating activities during FY 2016?

_____

_____

c. Which section of the statement would you look to for information on purchases of property and equipment? Did the organization spend more or less cash on purchases of property and equipment in FY 2016 than in FY 2015?

_____

_____

d. Which section of the statement would you look to for information on purchases of investments? Did the organization spend more or less cash on purchases of investments in FY 2016 than in FY 2015?

_____

_____

e. Is the organization's cash position better or worse on December 31, 2016 versus December 31, 2015?

_____

_____

6. And do not forget the footnotes:
   a. Where can you find information regarding all the significant accounting policies used by the organization?

_____

_____

   b. Which footnotes discuss the new accounting pronouncement adopted during FY 2016 related to the investments?

_____

_____

   c. What portion of the investment return for FY 2016 is related to realized losses? Where do you find this information?

_____

_____

   d. What portion of the investment return for FY 2016 is related to unrealized losses? Where do you find this information?

_____

_____

7. Among the most important issues revealed by the financial statements are the following:

_____

_____

Exercise 1A: Answers

1. Begin by looking at the independent auditor's report:
   a. What type of opinion is this?

   Unmodified opinion on comparative financial statements.

   b. What period is covered by the report?

   The years ended December 31, 2016 and 2015.

2. Locate the (1) Statements of Financial Position, (2) Statements of Activities, and (3) Statements of Cash Flows:
   a. How much are total current assets on December 31, 2016?

   $50,391,067.

   b. How much are total noncurrent assets on December 31, 2016?

   $89,820,461.

   c. How much are total liabilities on December 31, 2016?

   $71,033,113.

   d. How much are total unrestricted net assets on December 31, 2016?

   $69,178,415.

   e. What is the organization's change in net assets (bottom line) for the organization's year that ended on December 31, 2016 (FY 2016)?

   $(13,879,281).

3. Focusing on the Statements of Financial Position:
   a. Has the organization's current ratio (current assets/current liabilities) improved or declined from FY 2015 to FY 2016?

   It declined from .74 for FY 2015 to .71 for FY 2016. The current ratio is calculated by dividing the current assets by the current liabilities.

   b. How much does the organization have in long-term investments on December 31, 2016?

   $44,849,774.

   c. How much are total prepaid expenses—annual meeting?

   $16,395,499 (current portion of $16,288,599 plus noncurrent portion of $106,900).

   d. What is the allowance for uncollectible accounts receivable on December 31, 2016?

   $23,829.

   e. What is the organization's largest liability?

   Deferred revenue.

4. Moving to the Statements of Activities:

    a. How does the change in unrestricted net assets from operations for FY 2016 compare to those for FY 2015?

    The change in unrestricted net assets from operations has declined from an increase of $13,435,432 in FY 2015 to a decrease of $(516,379) in FY 2016. Revenues decreased 12 percent while expenses increased 4 percent.

    b. What is the key source of revenue?

    Annual meeting.

    c. What was the amount of the change in net assets from operations for the year that ended on December 31, 2016?

    A decrease of $(516,379).

    d. What was the net investment return for FY 2016 versus FY 2015?

    The organization experienced negative net investment return in the amount of ($13,362,902) for FY 2016 compared to a positive net investment return in the amount of $2,884,198 in FY 2015. This information appears in the statements of activities and in Note 3 in our example.

    e. What was the amount of the change in net assets for FY 2016 versus the amount of the change in net assets for FY 2015?

    Change in net assets for FY 2016 was a negative ($13,879,281) compared to a positive change in net assets for FY 2015 in the amount of $16,319,630.

5. On to the Statements of Cash Flows:

    a. What method of presentation did the organization use for the statement?

    Indirect method.

    b. What was the amount of cash and cash equivalents provided by or used in operating activities during FY 2016?

    The cash provided by operating activities was $6,454,226.

    c. Which section of the statement would you look to for information on purchases of property and equipment? Did the organization spend more or less cash on purchases of property and equipment in FY 2016 than in FY 2015?

    Cash flows from investing activities. The organization spent less cash on purchases of property and equipment in FY 2016 than FY 2015. The organization used cash of $1,301,002 in FY 2016 and $6,194,088 in FY 2015.

    d. Which section of the statement would you look to for information on purchases of investments? Did the organization spend more or less cash on purchases of investments in FY 2016 than in FY 2015?

    Cash flows from investing activities. The organization spent more on purchases of investments in FY 2016. The organization used cash of $74,168,305 in FY 2016 and $30,839,230 in FY 2015.

e. Is the organization's cash position better or worse on December 31, 2016 versus December 31, 2015?

The cash position is better in 2016. It increased by $1,478,602.

6. And do not forget the footnotes:
   a. Where can you find information regarding all the significant accounting policies used by the organization?

   In the summary of accounting policies at the beginning of the footnotes.

   b. Which footnotes discuss the new accounting pronouncement adopted during FY 2016 related to the investments?

   In the recent accounting pronouncements adopted in the summary of accounting policies and Note 2.

   c. What portion of the investment return for FY 2016 is related to realized losses? Where do you find this information?

   $4,743,114 of realized losses per Note 3.

   d. What portion of the investment return for FY 2016 is related to unrealized losses? Where do you find this information?

   $10,670,481 of unrealized losses per Note 3.

7. Among the most important issues revealed by the financial statements are the following:
   - *The dependence of the organization on a single source of revenue, the annual meeting, is a serious concern. It is clear that the organization would do well to diversify its revenue streams in a substantial manner. The fact that revenues from the meeting declined by more than $10M while expenses increased by $3.2M is quite disconcerting. This situation is critical to resolve given the organization's dependence on the annual meeting as a source of both gross and net income.*
   - *While the net investment loss was the most obvious blow to the financial strength of the organization, it was the result of a diversified portfolio being hit by unusually severe fluctuations in the market. A diversified investment portfolio has generally proven to be a good policy for assets that are being held for the long term. Thus, any major change in this area should be undertaken only with professional advice.*
   - *The organization appears to have a liquidity problem since in both years current liabilities are in the range of $20M greater than current assets. This is mitigated in part by the existence of the money market and mutual funds being held as part of the long-term investments. However, if cash were needed on an emergency basis, the sale of these liquid assets could be forced while in a down market. The organization would do well to have borrowing capacity available in the form of a line-of-credit to see it through any such emergency.*
   - *The organization cannot manage the return on investments as well as it can manage the income from operations ((decrease) increase in unrestricted net assets from operations). This is one of the major reasons the organization has chosen to present the investment return as a nonoperating activity in the statements of activities. The fact that the change in net assets from operations went from 15 percent of total revenue to less than 1 percent is among the single gravest issues to be dealt with. Both management and leadership should focus on improving this important figure.*

Example 1B

Society of American Associations

After Adoption of ASU 2016-14

Financial Statements

Years Ended December 31, 2016 and 2015

Example 1B

Society of American Associations

Independent Auditor's Report

To the Board of Directors of
Society of American Associations

Report on the Financial Statements

We have audited the accompanying statements of the **Society of American Associations** (the Society), which comprise the statements of financial position as of December 31, 2016 and 2015, and the related statements of activities and cash flows for the years then ended, and the related notes to the financial statements.

Management's Responsibility for the Financial Statements

Management is responsible for the preparation and fair presentation of these financial statements in accordance with accounting principles generally accepted in the United States of America; this includes the design, implementation, and maintenance of internal control relevant to the preparation and fair presentation of financial statements that are free from material misstatement, whether due to fraud or error.

Auditor's Responsibility

Our responsibility is to express an opinion on these financial statements based on our audits. We conducted our audits in accordance with auditing standards generally accepted in the United States of America. Those standards require that we plan and perform the audit to obtain reasonable assurance about whether the financial statements are free from material misstatement.

An audit involves performing procedures to obtain audit evidence about the amounts and disclosures in the financial statements. The procedures selected depend on the auditor's judgment, including the assessment of the risks of material misstatement of the financial statements, whether due to fraud or error. In making those risk assessments, the auditor considers internal control relevant to the entity's preparation and fair presentation of the financial statements in order to design audit procedures that are appropriate in the circumstances, but not for the purpose of expressing an opinion on the effectiveness of the entity's internal control. Accordingly, we express no such opinion. An audit also includes evaluating the appropriateness of accounting policies used and the reasonableness of significant accounting estimates made by management, as well as evaluating the overall presentation of the financial statements.

We believe that the audit evidence we have obtained is sufficient and appropriate to provide a basis for our audit opinion.

Example 1B

Society of American Associations

Opinion

In our opinion, the financial statements referred to above present fairly, in all material respects, the financial position of the **Society of American Associations** as of December 31, 2016 and 2015, and the changes in its net assets and its cash flows for the years then ended, in accordance with accounting principles generally accepted in the United States of America.

February 14, 2017

Example 1B

Entity uses a classified presentation which shows current and noncurrent assets and liabilities.

Society of American Associations

Statements of Financial Position

December 31,	2016	2015
Assets		
Current assets		
Cash and cash equivalents	$ 31,830,448	$ 30,351,846
Accounts receivable—net of allowance for uncollectible accounts of $23,829 in 2016 and 2015	1,448,668	7,694,031
Prepaid expenses—annual meeting	16,288,599	16,702,264
Prepaid expenses and other assets	823,352	680,338
Total current assets	50,391,067	55,428,479
Noncurrent assets		
Long-term investments	44,849,774	56,534,947
Property and equipment, net	44,863,787	45,186,925
Prepaid expenses—annual meeting—net of current portion	106,900	363,945
Total noncurrent assets	89,820,461	102,085,817
Total assets	$ 140,211,528	$ 157,514,296
Liabilities and Net Assets		
Current liabilities		
Accounts payable	$ 4,770,576	$ 5,528,746
Accrued expenses	4,756,708	3,272,547
Deferred revenue	61,505,829	65,655,307
Total current liabilities	71,033,113	74,456,600
Commitments and contingencies		
Net assets without donor restrictions	69,178,415	83,057,696
Total liabilities and net assets	$ 140,211,528	$ 157,514,296

Entity only has net assets without donor restrictions.

See accompanying summary of accounting policies and notes to financial statements.

Shaded lines indicate the basic totals that must be presented.

Example 1B

Society of American Associations

Statements of Activities

Years ended December 31,	2016	2015
Revenues		
Annual meeting	$ 68,083,991	$ 78,701,680
Membership dues	3,791,142	3,760,127
Meetings and conferences	2,194,980	2,065,282
Fees and assessments	1,008,227	1,061,717
Publication sales	826,890	1,078,996
Other income	62,185	42,149
Total revenues	75,967,415	86,709,951
Expenses		
Program services		
Annual meeting	38,937,135	35,737,453
Communications	8,591,621	8,274,453
Government and legal affairs	6,069,584	5,370,725
Member relations and customer service	5,244,459	5,458,744
Meetings and conferences	4,209,099	4,170,591
Technology and standards	3,122,172	3,014,999
Market research	2,807,570	3,105,830
Total program services	68,981,640	65,132,795
Supporting services		
General and administrative	7,502,154	8,141,724
Total expenses	76,483,794	73,274,519
(Decrease) increase in net assets without donor restrictions from operations	(516,379)	13,435,432
Nonoperating activities		
Investment return, net	(13,362,902)	2,884,198
Change in net assets	(13,879,281)	16,319,630
Net assets without donor restrictions, beginning of year	83,057,696	66,738,066
Net assets without donor restrictions, end of year	$ 69,178,415	$ 83,057,696

> Entity chose to show nonoperating items.

See accompanying summary of accounting policies and notes to financial statements.

Example 1B

Society of American Associations

Statements of Cash Flows

Years ended December 31,	2016	2015
Cash flows from operating activities		
Cash received from service recipients	$ 82,669,299	$ 89,789,376
Cash paid to employees and retirees	(25,682,916)	(23,791,822)
Cash paid to suppliers	(53,058,521)	(57,098,496)
Interest and dividends received	2,506,328	3,634,504
Other receipts	20,036	23,978
Net cash provided by operating activities	6,454,226	12,557,540
Cash flows from investing activities		
Proceeds from sale of investments	70,439,883	22,064,663
Purchases of investments	(74,168,305)	(30,839,230)
Proceeds from sales of property and equipment	53,800	-
Purchases of property and equipment	(1,301,002)	(6,194,088)
Net cash used in investing activities	(4,975,624)	(14,968,655)
Increase (decrease) in cash and cash equivalents	1,478,602	(2,411,115)
Cash and cash equivalents, beginning of year	30,351,846	32,762,961
Cash and cash equivalents, end of year	$ 31,830,448	$ 30,351,846

See accompanying summary of accounting policies and notes to financial statements.

Example 1B

Society of American Associations

Notes to Financial Statements

Summary of Accounting Policies:

Society

The Society of American Associations (the Society) is a tax-exempt trade association dedicated to the business interests of associations that operate in the United States. The majority of its revenue is derived from the annual meeting.

Basis of Accounting

The financial statements of the Society are presented in conformity with accounting principles generally accepted in the United States of America (U.S. GAAP) and have been prepared on the accrual basis of accounting.

Cash and Cash Equivalents

Cash and cash equivalents consist of highly liquid investments with original maturity dates of three months or less, excluding money market accounts held as part of long-term investments. The Society maintains cash balances which may exceed federally insured limits. The Society does not believe that this results in any significant credit risk.

Accounts Receivable

Accounts receivable consists primarily of amounts due from the sale of publications, advertising, and annual meeting registrations. The allowance method is used to determine the uncollectible amounts. The allowance is based upon prior years' experience and management's analysis of subsequent collections.

Allowances on accounts receivable are recorded when circumstances indicate collection is doubtful for particular accounts receivable or as a general reserve for all accounts receivable. Accounts receivable are written off if reasonable collection efforts prove unsuccessful. Bad debt expense is included in general and administrative expense in the statements of activities when allowances on accounts receivable are increased or when accounts written off exceed available allowances.

Prepaid Expenses: Annual Meeting

Prepaid expenses consist primarily of payments made by the Society to vendors in conjunction with the annual meeting which is held in May of each year. These payments are recognized as expenses in the year of the annual meeting.

Example 1B

Society of American Associations

Notes to Financial Statements

Long-term Investments

Investments in mutual funds are valued at fair value, based upon the net asset value per share as determined by quoted market prices. The preferred stock is valued based on market quotations from similar companies. The Society's investment in the venture capital fund has no readily determined market value and is valued at the net asset value per share practical expedient. Because of the inherent uncertainty of valuation, it is reasonably possible that such estimated values may differ significantly from the values that would have been used had a ready market for the securities existed, and the differences could be material.

Unrealized and realized gains and losses on investments are included in the accompanying statements of activities as nonoperating activity.

Property and Equipment

Property and equipment are stated at cost. The Society capitalizes all expenditures for property and equipment over $5,000. Depreciation and amortization are computed using the straight-line method over the estimated useful lives of the assets or the lesser of the minimum lease period or the asset's useful life for leasehold improvements. When assets are sold or otherwise disposed of, the asset and related accumulated depreciation and amortization are removed from the accounts, and any remaining gain or loss is included in operations. Repairs and maintenance are charged to expense when incurred.

Certain costs of internally developed software and website development are capitalized. The costs are being amortized over the estimated useful lives of the software and website.

Impairment of Long-Lived Assets

Management of the Society reviews asset carrying amounts whenever events or circumstances indicate that such carrying amounts may not be recoverable. When considered impaired, the carrying amount of the asset is reduced, by a charge to the statements of activities, to its current fair value.

Deferred Revenue

The Society defers amounts received in advance for the annual meeting and other meetings and conferences to be held in subsequent years. These receipts are recognized as income in the year the related meeting is held. Amounts received in 2016 and 2015 relating to deposits from exhibitors for the annual meeting to be conducted in 2017 and 2016 were $60,543,643 and $64,800,745, respectively. Amounts received for future annual meetings are included in deferred revenue in the accompanying statements of financial position.

Example 1B

Society of American Associations

Notes to Financial Statements

Net Assets Without Donor Restrictions

Net assets without donor restrictions are available for use in general operations.

Revenue Recognition

The annual meeting and other meetings and conferences revenue is recognized as revenue in the year the meeting or conference is held. Membership dues are recognized as revenue ratably over the calendar year membership term. Fees and assessments are recognized as revenue when the amounts are earned. Publication sales revenue is recognized at the time of sale.

Expenses

Expenses are recognized by the Society on an accrual basis. Expenses paid in advance and not yet incurred are recorded as prepaid until the applicable period.

Measure of Operations

For purposes of this presentation, the Society considers net investment return to be nonoperating.

Liquidity and Availability

The Society manages its liquid resources by focusing on investing excess cash in investments that maximize earnings potential balanced with the amount of risk the Society's Investment Committee has decided can be tolerated. The Society's investment policy is designed to ensure adequate financial assets are available to meet general expenditures, liabilities, and other obligations as they become due. The Society maintains easily liquidated investments in the long-term portfolio to meet its financial obligations. The Society focuses on collecting receivables timely to maximize the cash collections due to the Society. In addition, in order to manage the annual meeting each year the Society must make payments in advance to the meeting facility and vendors. The Society times these payments to maximize the time they have access to the cash.

> This example reflects the fact that the entity does not have any donor restricted funds.

The Society's financial assets available within one year of the statement of financial position date for general expenditure are as follows:

As of December 31, 2016,

Cash and cash equivalents	$ 31,830,448
Accounts receivable	1,448,668
Subtotal	33,279,116
Money market and mutual funds held in long-term portfolio	35,891,011
	$ 69,170,127

Example 1B

Society of American Associations

Notes to Financial Statements

Functional Allocation of Expenses

The costs of providing various program and supporting activities have been summarized on a functional basis in the statements of activities. Accordingly, certain costs have been allocated among the programs and supporting services benefited. The presentation of expenses by function and nature is included in Note 7.

New disclosure regarding the allocation of costs per ASU 2016-14.

The Society charges direct expenses incurred for a specific function directly to the program or supporting service category. These costs are those that can be specifically identified as being incurred for the activities of that program or supporting service. Other costs that are incurred by the Society benefit more than one program or supporting service and are allocated on a reasonable basis that is consistently applied. Expenses allocated based on square footage include occupancy charges, building operations, technology, and depreciation and amortization. Salaries and benefits, not directly charged, are allocated on the basis of estimates of time and effort. The Society reevaluates its allocation method each year to determine if there are adjustments that are necessary to the allocation method based on actual activities conducted during the year.

Financial Instruments

Financial instruments which potentially subject the Society to concentrations of credit risk consist principally of cash and cash equivalents and investments held at creditworthy financial institutions. At times the Society's operating cash accounts exceed the federally insured limit. The credit risk with respect to accounts receivable is limited because the Society deals with a large number of members and customers in a wide geographic area.

Use of Estimates

The preparation of financial statements in conformity with accounting principles generally accepted in the United States of America requires management to make estimates and assumptions that affect the reported amounts of assets and liabilities, disclosure of contingent assets and liabilities at the date of the financial statements, and the reported amounts of revenues and expenses during the reporting period. Actual results could differ from those estimates.

Advertising Costs

The Society expenses advertising costs as incurred. For the years ended December 31, 2016 and 2015, the Society expensed advertising costs of $5,573,779 and $4,837,601, respectively.

Recent Accounting Pronouncements Adopted

The Society adopted the Financial Accounting Standards Board (FASB) Accounting Standards Update (ASU) 2016-14, "Not-for-Profit Entities (Topic 958): Presentation of Financial Statements of Not-for-Profit Entities" for fiscal year ended December 31, 2016. The adoption of this ASU had no effect on net assets or the change in net assets presented for the years ended December 31, 2016 and 2015.

Example 1B

Society of American Associations

Notes to Financial Statements

In May 2015, the FASB issued ASU 2015-07, "Disclosure for Investments in Certain Entities that Calculate Net Asset Value per Share," which eliminates the requirement to categorize investments in the fair value hierarchy if their fair value is measured at net asset value per share (or its equivalent). ASU 2015-07 is effective for fiscal years beginning after December 15, 2016 with early adoption permitted. The Society chose to adopt the provisions of ASU 2015-07 early and updated disclosures are reflected in these statements. Other than the changes in the disclosures outlined above, there was no effect on the Society's financial statements as a result of adoption.

Recent Accounting Pronouncements to be Adopted

In May 2014, the FASB issued ASU 2014-09, "Revenue from Contracts with Customers (Topic 606)," which is a comprehensive new revenue recognition standard that will supersede existing revenue recognition guidance. The core principle of the guidance is that an entity should recognize revenue to depict the transfer of promised goods or services to customers in an amount that reflects the consideration to which the entity expects to be entitled in exchange for those goods or services. FASB issued ASU 2015-14 that deferred the effective date until annual periods beginning after December 15, 2018. Earlier adoption is permitted subject to certain limitations. The amendments in this update are required to be applied retrospectively to each prior reporting period presented or with the cumulative effect being recognized at the date of initial application. Management is currently evaluating the impact of this ASU on its financial statements.

In February 2016, the FASB issued ASU 2016-02, "Leases (Topic 842)," to increase transparency and comparability among organizations by recognizing lease assets and lease liabilities on the statement of financial position and disclosing key information about leasing arrangements for lessees and lessors. The new standard applies a right-of-use (ROU) model that requires, for all leases with a lease term of more than 12 months, an asset representing its right to use the underlying asset for the lease term and a liability to make lease payments to be recorded. The ASU is effective for fiscal years beginning after December 15, 2019 with early adoption permitted. Management is currently evaluating the impact of this ASU on its financial statements.

Example 1B

Society of American Associations

Notes to Financial Statements

1. Tax Status

The Society has been granted exemption by the Internal Revenue Service (IRS) from Federal income taxes under Section 501(c)(6) of the Internal Revenue Code. However, income from certain activities not directly related to the Society's tax-exempt purpose is subject to taxation as unrelated income. The Society earns unrelated business income on advertising revenue. The Society reported no unrelated business income tax expense for the years ended December 31, 2016 and 2015.

Management believes it has no material uncertain tax positions or any related penalties and interest to accrue for the years ended December 31, 2016 and 2015. The Society is still open to examination by taxing authorities from year 2013 forward.

2. Fair Value Measurements

U.S. GAAP establishes a common definition for fair value to be applied under generally accepted accounting principles requiring use of fair value, establishes a framework for measuring fair value, and expands disclosure about such fair value measurements.

U.S. GAAP defines fair value as the price that would be received to sell an asset or paid to transfer a liability (i.e., the "exit price") in an orderly transaction between market participants at the measurement date. Measurement date is the date of the financial statements. U.S. GAAP establishes a hierarchy for inputs used in measuring fair value that maximizes the use of observable inputs and minimizes the use of unobservable inputs by requiring that observable inputs be used when available.

Observable inputs are inputs that market participants would use in pricing the asset or liability developed based on market data obtained from sources independent of the Society. Unobservable inputs are inputs that reflect the Society's estimates about the assumptions market participants would use in pricing the asset or liability developed based on the best information available under the circumstances.

The hierarchy is broken down into three levels based on the reliability of the inputs as follows:

Level 1: Valuation based on quoted market prices in active markets for identical assets or liabilities. Since valuations are based on quoted prices that are readily and regularly available in an active market, valuation of these products does not entail a significant degree of judgment.

Example 1B

Society of American Associations

Notes to Financial Statements

Level 2: Valuation based on quoted market prices of investments that are not actively traded or for which certain significant inputs are not observable, either directly or indirectly.

Level 3: Valuation based on inputs that are unobservable and significant to the overall fair value measurement.

The following is a description of the valuation methodologies used for assets measured at fair value. There have been no changes in the methodologies used at December 31, 2016 and 2015.

The money market funds, fixed income mutual funds, equity mutual funds, and balanced mutual funds are all valued at the net asset value of the fund as published at December 31, 2016 and 2015.

Preferred stock is valued using market quotations from similar companies to estimate the fair value.

The Society's alternative investment is a venture capital fund which is valued based on level 3 inputs within the investment hierarchy used in measuring fair value. Given the absence of market quotations, the fair value is estimated using the net asset value (NAV) per share provided to the Society by the investment firm. This NAV is used as a practical expedient. Individual holdings within the alternative investment may include investment in both nonmarketable and market-traded securities. Nonmarketable securities may include equity in private companies, real estate, thinly traded securities, and other investment vehicles. While the venture capital fund contains varying degrees of risk, the Society's exposure with respect to this investment is limited to its carrying amount (fair value as described above).

Example 1B

Society of American Associations

Notes to Financial Statements

The table below sets forth those assets measured at fair value as of December 31, 2016.

| | Fair value measurement at reporting date using | | | |
Description	Quoted prices in active markets for identical assets (level 1)	Significant other observable inputs (level 2)	Significant other unobservable inputs (level 3)	Balance as of December 31, 2016
Money market funds	$ 2,936,095	$ -	$ -	$ 2,936,095
Fixed income mutual funds	15,436,922	-	-	15,436,922
Equity mutual funds	15,209,336	-	-	15,209,336
Balanced mutual funds	2,308,658	-	-	2,308,658
Preferred stock	-	1,329,777	-	1,329,777
Total	$ 35,891,011	$ 1,329,777	$ -	37,220,788
Venture capital fund reported at net asset value*				7,628,986
Total				$ 44,849,774

* Certain investments that are measured at fair value using the net asset value per share (or its equivalent) practical expedient have not been categorized in the fair value hierarchy. The fair value amounts presented in this table are intended to permit reconciliation of the fair value hierarchy to the amounts presented in the accompanying statements of financial position.

Example 1B

Society of American Associations

Notes to Financial Statements

The table below sets forth those assets measured at fair value as of December 31, 2015.

	Fair value measurement at reporting date using			
Description	Quoted prices in active markets for identical assets (level 1)	Significant other observable inputs (level 2)	Significant other unobservable inputs (level 3)	Balance as of December 31, 2015
Money market funds	$ 225,282	$ -	$ -	$ 225,282
Fixed income mutual funds	13,775,000	-	-	13,775,000
Equity mutual funds	26,820,203	-	-	26,820,203
Balanced mutual funds	6,715,898	-	-	6,715,898
Preferred stock	-	599,999	-	599,999
Total	$ 47,536,383	$ 599,999	$ -	48,136,382
Venture capital fund reported at net asset value*				8,398,565
Total				$ 56,534,947

* Certain investments that are measured at fair value using the net asset value per share (or its equivalent) practical expedient have not been categorized in the fair value hierarchy. The fair value amounts presented in this table are intended to permit reconciliation of the fair value hierarchy to the amounts presented in the accompanying statements of financial position.

Example 1B

Society of American Associations

Notes to Financial Statements

The following table summarizes the change in the fair value for the Level 3 item for the years ended December 31, 2016 and 2015:

	Fair value measurement at reporting date using unobservable inputs (Level 3)
	Venture capital fund
Balance, January 1, 2015	$ 8,408,771
Total unrealized losses	(10,206)
Transfers (to) from other investments	-
Balance, December 31, 2015	8,398,565
Total unrealized losses	(769,579)
Transfers (to) from other investments	-
Balance, December 31, 2016	$ 7,628,986

The following table sets forth a summary of the Society's investment with a reported NAV for the year ended December 31, 2016.

Investment	Fair Value	Unfunded Commitments	Redemption Frequency	Notice Period
Venture Capital Fund	$ 7,628,986	$ -	Monthly	10 days

3. Investment Return

> Authors' Note: This disclosure related to investment return is no longer required after the adoption of ASU 2016-14, however, entities may decide to maintain this disclosure.

Investment (losses) gains consist of the following:

Years ended December 31,	2016	2015
Dividends and interest	$ 2,506,328	$ 3,634,504
Investment expenses provided by external investment advisors and allocated internal management costs	(455,635)	(546,175)
Unrealized losses on investments	(10,670,481)	(501,051)
Realized (losses) gains on investments	(4,743,114)	296,920
Total investment (losses) gains	$ (13,362,902)	$ 2,884,198

> If this information is disclosed, the description of investment expenses must coincide with ASU 2016-14.

Example 1B

Society of American Associations

Notes to Financial Statements

4. Property and Equipment

Property and equipment consists of the following at:

December 31,	2016	2015
Building and improvements	$ 38,597,469	$ 38,597,469
Computer software and hardware	2,158,515	3,750,184
Furniture and equipment	2,036,965	2,010,689
Telecommunications	748,851	748,851
Building improvements	5,807,311	4,876,329
	49,349,111	49,983,522
Less: accumulated depreciation and amortization	(4,485,324)	(4,796,597)
Total	$ 44,863,787	$ 45,186,925

Depreciation and amortization expense for the years ended December 31, 2016 and 2015 was $1,570,340 and $1,060,589, respectively.

Example 1B

Society of American Associations

Notes to Financial Statements

5. **Commitments and Contingencies**

Operating Leases

The Society has entered into certain noncancelable operating leases for equipment which expire on various dates through 2019. The following schedule reflects the future minimum lease payments under all operating lease agreements:

Years Ending December 31,	
2017	$ 33,342
2018	33,342
2019	5,557
Total	$ 72,241

Rent expense for the years ended December 31, 2016 and 2015 was $33,342.

Pending Litigation

The Society is subject to various legal proceedings and claims, including patent infringement and antitrust violations, in the ordinary course of its business affairs. The Society cannot reasonably estimate the outcomes of these proceedings, and the Society intends to continue to vigorously defend its position in these matters. In the opinion of management, the potential adverse impact of these legal proceedings and claims is insignificant to the financial statements of the Society.

Other

The Society is committed under agreements for annual meeting space for future years. The total commitment under the agreements is not determinable as it depends upon attendance and other unknown factors. In the event that the Society cancels the agreements, it has agreed to pay liquidating damages.

Example 1B

Society of American Associations

Notes to Financial Statements

6. Benefit Plan   *Employee 401(k) Plan*

The Society maintains, for the benefit of all its employees, a deferred compensation arrangement established under Section 401(k) of the Internal Revenue Code (IRC). Employees may defer a portion of their salary up to the maximum amount allowable under Section 415 of the IRC. In 2016 and 2015, the Society contributed 100% of a participant's first 6% of contributions. Participants are fully vested in all matching contributions. During 2016 and 2015, the Society's contributions to the 401(k) plan totaled $717,564 and $718,440, respectively.

7. Functional Expenses   The Society's schedule of functional expenses displays expenses by natural classification and by function for the year ended December 31, 2016. The Society has chosen to only show this information for the current year based on the transition option in ASU 2016-14 in the year of adoption.

> The Society chose to present the expense analysis required by ASU 2016-14 in the footnotes.

Example 1B

Society of American Associations

Notes to Financial Statements

Note. 7 (continued)

Schedule of Functional Expenses

Year ended December 31, 2016

	Program Services								Supporting Services	Total
	Annual Meeting	Communications	Government and Legal Affairs	Member Relations and Customer Service	Meetings and Conferences	Technology and Standards	Market Research	Total Program Services	General and Administrative	Total Expenses
Personnel										
Salaries and wages	$ 4,141,208	$ 3,042,669	$ 1,337,902	$ 2,224,506	$ 1,761,845	$ 1,687,430	$ 1,482,384	$ 15,677,944	$ 3,576,409	$ 19,254,353
Benefits and taxes	1,220,987	792,391	347,854	578,371	458,879	438,731	385,420	4,222,633	929,886	5,152,519
Total personnel	5,362,195	3,835,060	1,685,756	2,802,877	2,220,724	2,126,161	1,867,804	19,900,577	4,506,295	24,406,872
Consultant, Contractors, and Professional Services										
Venue consultants	6,501,547	-	-	-	-	-	-	6,501,547	-	6,501,547
Contractors	4,409,573	1,791,307	1,466,454	690,845	310,625	14,559	172,355	8,855,698	548,798	9,404,496
Legal	1,508,764	301,755	180,838	284,098	23,831	32,876	123,587	2,455,749	300,978	2,756,727
Total consultant, contractors, and professional services	12,419,884	2,093,062	1,647,292	974,943	334,456	47,435	295,922	17,812,994	849,776	18,662,770
Annual Meeting										
Annual meeting venue	6,797,443	-	-	-	-	-	-	6,797,443	-	6,797,443
Annual meeting food and beverage	2,409,786	-	-	-	-	-	-	2,409,786	-	2,409,786
Annual meeting travel	2,040,488	-	-	-	-	-	-	2,040,488	-	2,040,488
Annual meeting services	705,484	-	-	-	-	-	-	705,484	-	705,484
Total annual meeting	11,953,201	-	-	-	-	-	-	11,953,201	-	11,953,201
Building Operations and Maintenance										
Occupancy charge	830,004	604,132	264,092	415,002	339,547	339,425	301,451	3,093,653	679,094	3,772,747
Building operations	110,681	80,012	35,810	55,347	45,284	45,284	40,621	413,039	90,115	503,154
Total building operations and maintenance	940,685	684,144	299,902	470,349	384,831	384,709	342,072	3,506,692	769,209	4,275,901
Other Expenses										
Advertising	3,802,097	442,332	-	279,528	918,838	130,984	-	5,573,779	-	5,573,779
Printing, replication, and mailing	2,737,558	536,357	980,143	190,302	110,457	105,201	88,978	4,748,996	187,965	4,936,961
Service charges	175,691	386,060	455,021	21,790	52,295	12,984	19,898	1,123,739	243,098	1,366,837
Office supplies	672,913	203,852	569,304	17,215	17,528	34,093	20,214	1,535,119	287,987	1,823,106
Technology	355,816	132,486	229,438	243,363	2,574	14,098	13,064	990,839	349,876	1,340,715
Depreciation and amortization	381,879	214,172	131,697	189,075	133,961	138,009	125,987	1,314,780	255,560	1,570,340
Other miscellaneous expenses	135,216	64,096	71,031	55,017	33,435	128,498	33,631	520,924	52,388	573,312
Total other expenses	8,261,170	1,979,355	2,436,634	996,290	1,269,088	563,867	301,772	15,808,176	1,376,874	17,185,050
Total expenses	$ 38,937,135	$ 8,591,621	$ 6,069,584	$ 5,244,459	$ 4,209,099	$ 3,122,172	$ 2,807,570	$ 68,981,640	$ 7,502,154	$ 76,483,794

Example 1B

Society of American Associations

Notes to Financial Statements

8. **Subsequent Events**

The Society has evaluated subsequent events through February 14, 2017, which is the date the financial statements were available to be issued. There were no events that required adjustments to or disclosure in these financial statements.

Exercise 1B: Working with Financial Statements

Use the financial statements in Example 1B for the Society of American Associations to familiarize yourself with a basic nonprofit financial statement that presents full comparative information for two years. In this example, the organization has adopted the provisions of ASU 2016-14.

1. Begin by looking at the independent auditor's report:
   a. What type of opinion is this?

   _____

   _____

   b. What period is covered by the report?

   _____

   _____

2. Locate the (1) Statements of Financial Position, (2) Statements of Activities, and (3) Statements of Cash Flows:
   a. How much are total current assets on December 31, 2016?

   _____

   _____

   b. How much are total noncurrent assets on December 31, 2016?

   _____

   _____

   c. How much are total liabilities on December 31, 2016?

   _____

   _____

   d. How much are total net assets without donor restrictions on December 31, 2016?

   _____

   _____

   e. What is the organization's change in net assets (bottom line) for the organization's year that ended on December 31, 2016 (FY 2016)?

   _____

   _____

3. Focusing on the Statements of Financial Position:

 a. Has the organization's current ratio (current assets/current liabilities) improved or declined from FY 2015 to FY 2016?

 _____

 _____

 b. How much does the organization have in long-term investments on December 31, 2016?

 _____

 _____

 c. How much are total prepaid expenses—annual meeting?

 _____

 _____

 d. What is the allowance for uncollectible accounts receivable on December 31, 2016?

 _____

 _____

 e. What is the organization's largest liability?

 _____

 _____

4. Moving to the Statements of Activities:

 a. How does the change in net assets without donor restrictions from operations for FY 2016 compare to those for FY 2015?

 _____

 _____

 b. What is the key source of revenue?

 _____

 _____

 c. What was the amount of the increase or decrease in the change in net assets from operations for the year that ended on December 31, 2016?

 _____

 _____

 d. What was the net investment return for FY 2016 versus FY 2015?

 _____

 _____

e. What was the amount of the change in net assets without donor restrictions for FY 2016 versus the amount of the change in net assets without donor restrictions for FY 2015?

_____

_____

5. On to the Statements of Cash Flows:
   a. What method of presentation did the organization use for the statement?

_____

_____

   b. What was the amount of cash and cash equivalents provided by or used in operating activities during FY 2016?

_____

_____

   c. Which section of the statement would you look to for information on purchases of property and equipment? Did the organization spend more or less cash on purchases of property and equipment in FY 2016 than in FY 2015?

_____

_____

   d. Which section of the statement would you look to for information on purchases of investments? Did the organization spend more or less cash on purchases of investments in FY 2016 than in FY 2015?

_____

_____

   e. Is the organization's cash position better or worse on December 31, 2016 versus December 31, 2015?

_____

_____

6. And do not forget the footnotes:
   a. Where can you find information regarding all the significant accounting policies used by the organization?

_____

_____

   b. Which footnotes discuss the new accounting pronouncement adopted during FY 2016 related to the investments?

_____

_____

c. What portion of the investment return for FY 2016 is related to realized losses? Where do you find this information?

_____

_____

d. What portion of the investment return for FY 2016 is related to unrealized losses? Where do you find this information?

_____

_____

e. Where would you find information on the total financial assets available within one year of the Statements of Financial Position date for general expenditures?

_____

_____

f. What is the amount of the Society's financial assets available within one year of the Statements of Financial Position date for general expenditures?

_____

_____

7. Which components of the financial statements reflect the adoption of ASU 2016-14?

_____

_____

8. Among the most important issues revealed by the financial statements are the following:

_____

_____

Exercise 1B: Answers

1. Begin by looking at the independent auditor's report:
   a. What type of opinion is this?

   Unmodified opinion on comparative financial statements.

   b. What period is covered by the report?

   The years ended December 31, 2016 and 2015.

2. Locate the (1) Statements of Financial Position, (2) Statements of Activities, and (3) Statements of Cash Flows:
   a. How much are total current assets on December 31, 2016?

   $50,391,067.

   b. How much are total noncurrent assets on December 31, 2016?

   $89,820,461.

   c. How much are total liabilities on December 31, 2016?

   $71,033,113.

   d. How much are total net assets without donor restrictions on December 31, 2016?

   $69,178,415.

   e. What is the organization's change in net assets (bottom line) for the organization's year that ended on December 31, 2016 (FY 2016)?

   $(13,879,281).

3. Focusing on the Statements of Financial Position
   a. Has the organization's current ratio (current assets/current liabilities) improved or declined from FY 2015 to FY 2016?

   It declined from .74 for FY 2015 to .71 for FY 2016. The current ratio is calculated by dividing the current assets by the current liabilities.

   b. How much does the organization have in long-term investments on December 31, 2016?

   $44,849,774.

   c. How much are total prepaid expenses—annual meeting?

   $16,395,499 (current portion of $16,288,599 plus noncurrent portion of $106,900).

   d. What is the allowance for uncollectible accounts receivable on December 31, 2016?

   $23,829.

   e. What is the organization's largest liability?

   Deferred revenue.

4. Moving to the Statements of Activities:

    a. How does the change in net assets without donor restrictions from operations for FY 2016 compare to those for FY 2015?

    The change in net assets without donor restrictions from operations has declined from an increase of $13,435,432 in FY 2015 to a decrease of $(516,379) in FY 2016. Revenues decreased 12 percent while expenses increased 4 percent.

    b. What is the key source of revenue?

    Annual meeting.

    c. What was the amount of the increase or decrease in the change in net assets from operations for the year that ended on December 31, 2016?

    A decrease of $(516,379).

    d. What was the net investment return for FY 2016 versus FY 2015?

    The organization experienced negative net investment return in the amount of ($13,362,902) for FY 2016 compared to a positive net investment return in the amount of $2,884,198 in FY 2015. This information appears in the statements of activities and in Note 3 in our example.

    e. What was the amount of the change in net assets without donor restrictions for FY 2016 versus the amount of the change in net assets without donor restrictions for FY 2015?

    Change in net assets without donor restrictions for FY 2016 was a negative ($13,879,281) compared to a positive change in net assets without donor restrictions for FY 2015 in the amount of $16,319,630.

5. On to the Statements of Cash Flows:

    a. What method of presentation did the organization use for the statement?

    Direct method.

    b. What was the amount of cash and cash equivalents provided by or used in operating activities during FY 2016?

    The cash provided by operating activities was $6,454,226.

    c. Which section of the statement would you look to for information on purchases of property and equipment? Did the organization spend more or less cash on purchases of property and equipment in FY 2016 than in FY 2015?

    Cash flows from investing activities. The organization spent less cash on purchases of property and equipment in FY 2016 than FY 2015. The organization used cash of $1,301,002 in FY 2016 and $6,194,088 in FY 2015.

    d. Which section of the statement would you look to for information on purchases of investments? Did the organization spend more or less cash on purchases of investments in FY 2016 than in FY 2015?

      Cash flows from investing activities. The organization spent more on purchases of investments in FY 2016. The organization used cash of $74,168,305 in FY 2016 and $30,839,230 in FY 2015.

    e. Is the organization's cash position better or worse on December 31, 2016 versus December 31, 2015?

      The cash position is better in 2016. It increased by $1,478,602.

6. And do not forget the footnotes:

    a. Where can you find information regarding all the significant accounting policies used by the organization?

      In the summary of accounting policies at the beginning of the footnotes.

    b. Which footnotes discuss the new accounting pronouncement adopted during FY 2016 related to the investments?

      In the recent accounting pronouncements in the summary of accounting policies and Note 2.

    c. What portion of the investment return for FY 2016 is related to realized losses? Where do you find this information? (As noted, once the entity adopts ASU 2016-14, this information will no longer be required to be disclosed. In our example, the disclosure was still provided, but it is not required.)

      $4,743,114 of realized losses per Note 3.

    d. What portion of the investment return for FY 2016 is related to unrealized losses? Where do you find this information? (As noted, once the entity adopts ASU 2016-14, this information will no longer be required to be disclosed. In our example, the disclosure was still provided, but it is not required.)

      $10,670,481 of unrealized losses per Note 3.

    e. Where would you find information on the total financial assets available within one year of the Statements of Financial Position date for general expenditures?

      In the summary of accounting policies note under the heading liquidity and availability.

    f. What is the amount of the Society's financial assets available within one year of the Statements of Financial Position date for general expenditures?

      $69,170,127.

7. Which components of the financial statements reflect the adoption of ASU 2016-14?

    • *Change in terminology from unrestricted net assets to net assets without donor restrictions.*

    • *Liquidity and Availability note in the Summary of Accounting Policies (the entity had already included this before the adoption but other entities may have not).*

    • *Functional allocation methodology for expenses is included in the Summary of Accounting Policies.*

- *The effect of adopting ASU 2016-14 is included in the Summary of Accounting Policies.*
- *The information in Note 3, Investment Return, could be removed as noted.*
- *The required analysis of expenses by function and nature was included as Note 7.*

8. Among the most important issues revealed by the financial statements are the following:

- *The dependence of the organization on a single source of revenue, the annual meeting, is a serious concern. It is clear that the organization would do well to diversify its revenue streams in a substantial manner. The fact that revenues from the meeting declined by more than $10M while expenses increased by $3.2M is quite disconcerting. This situation is critical to resolve given the organization's dependence on the annual meeting as a source of both gross and net income.*
- *While the net investment loss was the most obvious blow to the financial strength of the organization, it was the result of a diversified portfolio being hit by unusually severe fluctuations in the market. A diversified investment portfolio has generally proven to be a good policy for assets that are being held for the long term. Thus, any major change in this area should be undertaken only with professional advice.*
- *The organization appears to have a liquidity problem since in both years current liabilities are in the range of $20M greater than current assets. This is mitigated in part by the existence of the money market and mutual funds being held as part of the long-term investments. However, if cash were needed on an emergency basis, the sale of these liquid assets could be forced while in a down market. The organization would do well to have borrowing capacity available in the form of a line-of-credit to see it through any such emergency.*
- *The organization cannot manage the return on investments as well as it can manage the income from operations ((decrease) increase in net assets without donor restrictions from operations). This is one of the major reasons the organization has chosen to present the investment return as a nonoperating activity in the statements of activities. The fact that the change in net assets from operations went from 15 percent of total revenue to less than 1 percent is among the single gravest issues to be dealt with. Both management and leadership should focus on improving this important figure.*

CHAPTER 19

Example Set 2

The following examples present the financial statements of a charity, The United States Charity.

The statements reflect that the organization was established on June 15, 2015, and selected a December 31 fiscal year-end. As a result, the Statement of Activities for the year ended December 31, 2015, includes six and one half months of operations covering the period from June 15, 2015 (inception), through December 31, 2015. The Statement of Activities for the year ended December 31, 2016, is, as is typical, for a full 12-month period.

Because of the differences in the length of time covered in 2016 and 2015, and the fact that the organization only began its operations in the middle of 2015, comparing the revenue and expenses for the two periods must be done carefully.

The Statements of Financial Position are, like all such statements, as of the close of business on the final day of the fiscal year, which is December 31, 2016 and 2015.

Example 2A: Prepared using accounting guidance before the adoption of ASU 2016-14.

Example 2B: Prepared after the adoption of ASU 2016-14.

Example 2A

The United States Charity

Before the Adoption of ASU 2016-14

Financial Statements

For the year ended December 31, 2016 and the period from inception (June 15, 2015) through December 31, 2015

Example 2A

The United States Charity

Independent Auditor's Report

To the Board of Directors
The United States Charity

Report on the Financial Statements

We have audited the accompanying statements of **The United States Charity** (the Organization), which comprise the statements of financial position as of December 31, 2016 and 2015, and the related statements of activities and cash flows for the year ended December 31, 2016 and the period from inception (June 15, 2015) through December 31, 2015, and the related notes to the financial statements.

Management's Responsibility for the Financial Statements

Management is responsible for the preparation and fair presentation of these financial statements in accordance with accounting principles generally accepted in the United States of America; this includes the design, implementation, and maintenance of internal control relevant to the preparation and fair presentation of financial statements that are free from material misstatement, whether due to fraud or error.

Auditor's Responsibility

Our responsibility is to express an opinion on these financial statements based on our audits. We conducted our audits in accordance with auditing standards generally accepted in the United States of America. Those standards require that we plan and perform the audit to obtain reasonable assurance about whether the financial statements are free from material misstatement.

An audit involves performing procedures to obtain audit evidence about the amounts and disclosures in the financial statements. The procedures selected depend on the auditor's judgment, including the assessment of the risks of material misstatement of the financial statements, whether due to fraud or error. In making those risk assessments, the auditor considers internal control relevant to the entity's preparation and fair presentation of the financial statements in order to design audit procedures that are appropriate in the circumstances, but not for the purpose of expressing an opinion on the effectiveness of the entity's internal control. Accordingly, we express no such opinion. An audit also includes evaluating the appropriateness of accounting policies used and the reasonableness of significant accounting estimates made by management, as well as evaluating the overall presentation of the financial statements.

We believe that the audit evidence we have obtained is sufficient and appropriate to provide a basis for our audit opinion.

Example 2A

The United States Charity

Opinion

In our opinion, the financial statements referred to above present fairly, in all material respects, the financial position of **The United States Charity** as of December 31, 2016 and 2015, and the changes in its net assets and its cash flows for the year ended December 31, 2016 and for the period from inception (June 15, 2015) through December 31, 2015, in accordance with accounting principles generally accepted in the United States of America.

March 5, 2017

Example 2A

The United States Charity

Statements of Financial Position

December 31,		2016		2015
Assets				
Cash and cash equivalents	$	765,827	$	2,047,764
Grants and contributions receivable		1,750,679		1,000,000
Prepaid expenses		20,178		-
Fixed assets, net of accumulated depreciation and amortization		163,102		28,614
Investments		25,000		-
Deposits		30,379		6,000
Total assets	$	2,755,165	$	3,082,378
Liabilities and Net Assets				
Accounts payable and accrued expenses	$	606,228	$	479,843
Capital lease payable		131,620		-
Deferred rent liability		10,220		-
Total liabilities		748,068		479,843
Commitments and contingencies				
Net assets				
Unrestricted		257,097		300,175
Temporarily restricted		1,750,000		2,302,360
Total net assets		2,007,097		2,602,535
Total liabilities and net assets	$	2,755,165	$	3,082,378

The accompanying notes are an integral part of these financial statements.

Shaded lines indicate the
basic totals that must
be presented.

Example 2A

This is the layered format for presenting net assets by type.

The United States Charity

Statements of Activities

For the year ended December 31, 2016/period from inception through December 31, 2015	2016	2015
Changes in Unrestricted Net Assets		
Revenue and support		
Grants and contributions	$ 2,560,000	$ 2,166,262
Investment return, net	21,548	30,653
Other income	141	223,312
Net assets released from time restrictions	2,302,360	-
Total revenue and support	4,884,049	2,420,227
Expenses		
Program services		
Information dissemination	2,866,720	1,202,758
Research	274,569	197,723
Total program services	3,141,289	1,400,481
Supporting services		
General and administrative	1,102,369	715,540
Fundraising	683,469	4,031
Total supporting services	1,785,838	719,571
Total expenses	4,927,127	2,120,052
Change in unrestricted net assets	(43,078)	300,175
Changes in Temporarily Restricted Net Assets		
Grants and contributions	1,750,000	2,302,360
Net assets released from time restrictions	(2,302,360)	-
Change in temporarily restricted net assets	(552,360)	2,302,360
Change in net assets	(595,438)	2,602,535
Net assets, beginning of year/inception	2,602,535	-
Net assets, end of year/period	$ 2,007,097	$ 2,602,535

The accompanying notes are an integral part of these financial statements.

This entity has not elected the option to categorize any items as nonoperating.

Indirect
method of
presentation.

Example 2A

The United States Charity

Statements of Cash Flows

For the year ended December 31, 2016/period from inception through December 31, 2015		2016		2015
Cash flows from operating activities				
Change in net assets	$	(595,438)	$	2,602,535
Adjustments to reconcile change in net assets				
to net cash (used in) provided by operating activities				
Depreciation and amortization		13,036		2,930
Unrealized loss on investments		10,000		-
Loss on disposition of furniture and equipment		-		2,181
Changes in assets and liabilities				
Grants and contributions receivable		(750,679)		(1,000,000)
Prepaid expenses		(20,178)		-
Deposits		(24,379)		(6,000)
Accounts payable and accrued expenses		126,385		479,843
Deferred rent liability		10,220		-
Net cash (used in) provided by operating activities		(1,231,033)		2,081,489
Cash flows from investing activities				
Purchases of investments		(35,000)		-
Purchases of fixed assets		(13,373)		(33,725)
Net cash used in investing activities		(48,373)		(33,725)
Cash flows from financing activities				
Payments on capital lease		(2,531)		-
Net cash used in financing activities		(2,531)		-
(Decrease) increase in cash and cash equivalents		(1,281,937)		2,047,764
Cash and cash equivalents, beginning of year/inception		2,047,764		-
Cash and cash equivalents, end of year/period	$	765,827	$	2,047,764
Supplemental cash flow information				
Noncash investing and financing activities				
Leased property under capital lease	$	134,151	$	-
Interest paid	$	781	$	-

The accompanying notes are an integral part of these financial statements.

Example 2A

The United States Charity

Notes to Financial Statements

1. Organization and Summary of Significant Accounting Policies

Organization

The United States Charity(the Organization) was incorporated on June 15, 2015under the laws of the Districtof Columbia as a nonprofit organization. The Organization's goal is to be the nation's sole source of guidance for fundraising professionals. The Organization's activities are funded primarily through grants and contributions from foundations and corporations.

Basis of Accounting

The Organization's financial statements are presented in conformity with accounting principles generally accepted in the United States of America (U.S. GAAP) and have been prepared on the accrual basis of accounting.

Cash and Cash Equivalents

The Organization considers all deposits in banks to be cash equivalents. The cash and cash equivalents of the Organization are composed of amounts in accounts at banks.

Concentration of Credit Risk

The cash and cash equivalents of the Organization are composed of amounts in accounts at banks. While the amounts at times exceed the amount guaranteed by federal agencies and therefore bear some risk, the Organization has not experienced any loss of funds. As of December 31, 2016 and 2015 , the amount in excess of the amount guaranteed by federal agencies was $469,666 and $2,080,459, respectively.

Fixed Assets

Furniture and equipment are stated at cost and are depreciated on a straight-line basis over the estimated useful lives of the respective assets, which range from three to five years. Leasehold improvements are amortized over the lesser of the estimated useful life of the asset or the remaining lease term. The asset and liability under the capital lease are recorded at the lower of the present value of the minimum lease payments or the fair value of the asset. The capital lease assets are amortized over the lower of the related lease term or their estimated useful life. Amortization of assets under the capital lease is included in depreciation and amortization expense for 2016. Expenditures for major repairs and improvements are capitalized. Expenditures for minor repairs and maintenance costs are expensed when incurred. Upon retirement or disposal of assets, the accounts are relieved of the cost and accumulated depreciation and amortization, with any resulting gain or loss included in revenue or expense.

Example 2A

The United States Charity

Notes to Financial Statements

The Organization capitalizes all expenditures for furniture and equipment and leasehold improvements over $250.

Investments

During the year ended December 31, 2016 the Organization invested $35,000 in institutional commingled funds that have no readily determinable market value and are valued at fair value as estimated by the fund. Because of the inherent uncertainty of valuation, it is reasonably possible that estimated values may differ from values that would have been used had a ready market for the securities existed. In addition, the fund may have risk associated with its concentrations in one geographic region and in certain industries.

Classification of Net Assets

The net assets of the Organization are reported as follows:

- Unrestricted net assets represent the portion of expendable funds that are available for support of the Organization's operations.

- Temporarily restricted net assets are specifically restricted by donors for various programs or future periods.

Revenue Recognition

Grants and contributions are reported as revenue in the year in which payments are received and/or unconditional promises are made. The Organization reports gifts of cash and other assets that are received with donor stipulations limiting the use of the donated assets as unrestricted support if all such donor restrictions are met in the year the award is received. Gifts of cash and other assets that are received with donor stipulations limiting the use of the donated assets are reported as temporarily restricted net assets if such donor stipulations are not fully met in the year the award is received. When a stipulated time restriction ends or purpose restriction is accomplished, temporarily restricted net assets are reclassified to unrestricted net assets and reported in the statements of activities as net assets released from restrictions.

Expenses

Expenses are recognized by the Organization on an accrual basis. Expenses paid in advance and not yet incurred are recorded as prepaid until the applicable period.

Example 2A

The United States Charity

Notes to Financial Statements

Liquidity and Availability

The Organization manages its liquid resources by focusing on fundraising efforts to ensure the entity has adequate contributions and grants to cover the programs that are being conducted. The Organization prepares very detailed budgets and has been very active in cutting costs to ensure the entity remains liquid.

As discussed in Note 10, the Organization maintains a line-of-credit to assist in meeting cash needs if they experience a lag between the receipt of contributions and grants and the payment of costs. This is a last resort option and the Organization did not have to use the line-of-credit during the year ended December 31, 2016 and the period from inception to December 31, 2015.

The following reflects the Organization's financial assets as of December 31, 2016 expected to be available within one year to meet the cash needs for general expenditures.

Cash and cash equivalents	$ 765,827
Grants and contributions receivable	1,750,679
	$ 2,516,506

The investments were not deemed to be available due to the nature of the investment and the lack of liquidity. The grants and contributions receivable are subject to implied time restrictions but are expected to be collected within one year.

Example 2A

The United States Charity

Notes to Financial Statements

<u>Estimates</u>

The preparation of financial statements in conformity with accounting principles generally accepted in the United States of America requires management to make estimates and assumptions that affect the reported amounts of assets and liabilities, disclosure of contingent assets and liabilities at the date of the financial statements, and the reported amounts of revenues and expenses during the reporting period. Accordingly, actual results could differ from those estimates.

<u>Functional Allocation of Expenses</u>

The costs of providing the various programs and other activities have been summarized on a functional basis in the accompanying statements of activities. Accordingly, certain costs have been allocated among the programs and supporting services benefited.

<u>Recent Accounting Pronouncements to be Adopted</u>

In May 2014, the Financial Accounting Standards Board (FASB) issued Accounting Standards Update (ASU) 2014-09, "Revenue from Contracts with Customers (Topic 606)," which is a comprehensive new revenue recognition standard that will supersede existing revenue recognition guidance. The core principle of the guidance is that an entity should recognize revenue to depict the transfer of promised goods or services to customers in an amount that reflects the consideration to which the entity expects to be entitled in exchange for those goods or services. FASB issued ASU 2015-14 that deferred the effective date until annual periods beginning after December 15, 2018. Earlier adoption is permitted subject to certain limitations. The amendments in this update are required to be applied retrospectively to each prior reporting period presented or with the cumulative effect being recognized at the date of initial application. Management is currently evaluating the impact of this ASU on its financial statements.

In February 2016, the FASB issued ASU 2016-02, "Leases (Topic 842)," to increase transparency and comparability among organizations by recognizing lease assets and lease liabilities on the statement of financial position and disclosing key information about leasing arrangements for lessees and lessors. The new standard applies a right-of-use (ROU) model that requires, for all leases with a lease term of more than 12 months, an asset representing its right to use the underlying asset for the lease term and a liability to make lease payments to be recorded. The ASU is effective for fiscal years beginning after December 15, 2019 with early adoption permitted. Management is currently evaluating the impact of this ASU on its financial statements.

Example 2A

The United States Charity

Notes to Financial Statements

In August 2016, the FASB issued ASU 2016-14, "Not-for-Profit Entities (Topic 958): Presentation of Financial Statements of Not-for-Profit Entities." The ASU amends the current reporting model for nonprofit organizations and enhances their required disclosures. The major changes include: (a) requiring the presentation of only two classes of net assets now entitled "net assets without donor restrictions" and "net assets with donor restrictions," (b) modifying the presentation of underwater endowment funds and related disclosures, (c) requiring the use of the placed-in-service approach to recognize the expirations of restrictions on gifts used to acquire or construct long-lived assets absent explicit donor stipulations otherwise, (d) requiring that all nonprofits present an analysis of expenses by function and nature in either the statement of activities, a separate statement, or in the notes and disclose a summary of the allocation methods used to allocate costs, (e) requiring the disclosure of quantitative and qualitative information regarding liquidity and availability of resources, (f) presenting investment return net of external and direct internal investment expenses, and (g) modifying other financial statement reporting requirements and disclosures intended to increase the usefulness of nonprofit financial statements. The ASU is effective for the financial statements for fiscal years beginning after December 15, 2017. Early adoption is permitted. The provisions of the ASU must be applied on a retrospective basis for all years presented although certain optional practical expedients are available for periods prior to adoption. Management is currently evaluating the impact of this ASU on its financial statements.

2. Grants and Contributions Receivable

Grants and contributions receivable of $1,750,679 and $1,000,000 at December 31, 2016 and 2015, respectively, includes grants and contributions from foundations for general support in the coming years. All contributions are due to be received within one year and are considered fully collectible.

3. Fair Value Measurements

The investment in commingled funds is stated at fair value of $25,000 based on the value as estimated by the fund manager and evaluated by management at December 31, 2016. Investment return consists of interest income of $31,548 and an unrealized loss on the commingled funds of $10,000. There were no external fees incurred related to this investment.

The Organization follows U.S. GAAP which establishes a common definition for fair value to be applied under generally accepted accounting principles requiring use of fair value, establishes a framework for measuring fair value, and expands disclosures about such fair value measurements.

Example 2A

The United States Charity

Notes to Financial Statements

U.S. GAAP defines fair value as the price that would be received to sell an asset or paid to transfer a liability (i.e., the "exit price") in an orderly transaction between market participants at the measurement date. Measurement date is the date of the financial statements. U.S. GAAP establishes a hierarchy for inputs used in measuring fair value that maximizes the use of observable inputs and minimizes the use of unobservable inputs by requiring that observable inputs be used when available.

Observable inputs are inputs that market participants would use in pricing the asset or liability developed based on market data obtained from sources independent of the Organization. Unobservable inputs are inputs that reflect the Organization's estimates about the assumptions market participants would use in pricing the asset or liability developed based on the best information available under the circumstances.

The hierarchy is broken down into three levels based on the reliability of the inputs as follows:

Level 1: Valuation based on quoted market prices in active markets for identical assets or liabilities. Since valuations are based on quoted prices that are readily and regularly available in an active market, valuation of these products does not entail a significant degree of judgment.

Level 2: Valuation based on quoted market prices of investments that are not actively traded or for which certain significant inputs are not observable, either directly or indirectly.

Level 3: Valuation based on inputs that are unobservable and significant to the overall fair value measurement.

All of the Organization's assets are classified as Level 3 in the fair value hierarchy.

The following table sets forth a summary of the changes in the fair value of the Organization's level 3 assets for the year ended December 31, 2016:

Level 3 Assets:

Balance, beginning of year	$ -
Purchases	35,000
Unrealized loss	(10,000)
Balance, end of year	$ 25,000

Example 2A

The United States Charity

Notes to Financial Statements

4. **Temporarily Restricted Net Assets**

Temporarily restricted net assets of $1,750,000 and $2,302,360 as of December 31, 2016 and 2015, respectively, are for general operations but designated by third-party donors for use during the years ending December 31, 2017 and December 31, 2016, respectively, so they are subject only to time restrictions.

5. **Contributed Services**

During the year ended December 31, 2016 there were no contributed services and materials. During the period from inception through December 31, 2015, the Organization received donated services totaling $223,312 representing the fair value of these goods and services. Such donations included $11,312 of donated consulting fees and $12,000 of donated professional services and $200,000 of donated office space. Donated contributions have been recorded as other income in the accompanying statements of activities. Donated consulting and professional fees are included in general and administrative expense in the accompanying statements of activities. The donated office space expense was allocated among the programs and supporting services benefited based on square footage.

6. **Income Taxes**

Under Section 501(c)(3) of the Internal Revenue Code, the Organization is exempt from federal taxes on income other than net unrelated business income. For the year ended December 31, 2016 and the period from inception through December 31, 2015, no provision for income taxes was made as the Organization had no net unrelated business income.

Management believes it has no material uncertain tax positions or any related penalties and interest to accrue for the year ended December 31, 2016 and the period from inception through December 31, 2015. The Organization is still open to examination by taxing authorities from 2015 forward.

Example 2A

The United States Charity

Notes to Financial Statements

7. Fixed Assets

The following is a summary of fixed assets at December 31:

Year/period ended December 31,	2016	2015
Furniture and equipment	$ 38,537	$ 31,416
Leased property under capital lease	134,151	-
Leasehold improvements	6,252	-
Subtotal	178,940	31,416
Less allowance for depreciation and amortization	(15,838)	(2,802)
Fixed assets, net	$ 163,102	$ 28,614

Depreciation and amortization expense for the year ended December 31, 2016 and the period from inception through December 31, 2015 were $13,036 and $2,930, respectively.

8. Capital Lease

The Organization has entered into a master lease agreement with a financial institution to finance certain office equipment, furniture, and leasehold improvement additions. Under the terms of the master lease agreement there are two separate schedules that provide for the repayment of the amounts financed over the life of the assets purchased that expire in 2019 and 2021. The master lease agreement is secured by the assets purchased.

The following is an analysis of the leased property under the capital lease by major classes:

Asset balances at December 31, 2016	
Classes of property:	
Furniture and equipment	$ 118,330
Leasehold improvements	15,821
Subtotal	134,151
Less accumulated amortization	(2,895)
Total	$ 131,256

Example 2A

The United States Charity

Notes to Financial Statements

Minimum future lease payments under the capital lease master agreement as of December 31, 2016 through expiration are:

Years ending December 31,		
2017	$	39,751
2018		39,751
2019		37,920
2020		17,780
2021		16,299
Total minimum lease payments		151,501
Less amount representing interest		(19,881)
Present value of net minimum lease payments	$	131,620

The interest rate on the master lease is 7%, and is imputed based on the lower of the Organization's incremental borrowing rate at the inception of the leases or the lessor's implicit rate of return.

9. Lease Commitment

In January 2016, the Organization entered into a lease for office space. The lease term commenced on January 1, 2016 and will expire on January 31, 2020. The lease provides for scheduled annual rent increases of 3%. In accordance with U.S. GAAP rent expense is recorded monthly on a straight-line basis in the amount of $19,493. This resulted in a deferred rent liability as of December 31, 2016 in the amount of $10,220. Rental expense for the year ended December 31, 2016 was $233,920.

The future minimum lease payments under this lease on an annual basis are as follows:

Years ending December 31,		
2017	$	240,940
2018		248,169
2019		255,614
2020		21,886
Total	$	766,609

Example 2A

The United States Charity

Notes to Financial Statements

10. Line-of-Credit

On December 15, 2015, the Organization entered into a line-of-credit, not to exceed $100,000. This line-of-credit bears interest at the Wall Street Journal prime rate of interest plus 1.5 percentage points, which was 4.75% at December 31, 2016 and 4.5% at December 31, 2015. The line-of-credit is secured by substantially all the assets of the Organization and contains restrictive financial covenants such as the use of proceeds, financial information, other debts and liens. As of December 31, 2016 and 2015, the Organization did not have an outstanding balance due on the line-of-credit.

11. Description of Program and Supporting Services

Information Dissemination

The Organization regularly monitors the activities of fundraising professionals to find ways to improve results and improve campaigns. This information is disseminated through various channels.

Research

The Organization works to compile high-quality measures and data that can be used to assess the progress of charity work throughout the nation.

General and Administrative

This supporting service category includes the functions necessary to secure proper administrative functioning of the Organization's governing board, maintain an adequate working environment, and manage financial responsibilities of the Organization.

Fundraising

This supporting service category includes expenditures which provide the structure necessary to encourage and secure private financial support. No fundraising costs are allocated to programs or supporting services.

Example 2A

The United States Charity

Notes to Financial Statements

12. **Management's Plans**   During the year ended December 31, 2016 the Organization had a decrease in net assets of approximately $595,000. Even with net assets available for use in 2017 of over $2 million, the Organization is acting to secure future funding, to carefully control and configure expenses, make programmatic progress and continue as a going concern.

Aggressive and diversified fundraising efforts are being pursued to increase contributed income during 2017 and beyond. Reduced expenditures are reflected in the 2017 budget going forward. As of the report date, the grants and contributions receivable shown in the December 31, 2016 statements of financial position, as well as new funding, have been received and cash balances are in excess of $2.1 million.

13. **Subsequent Events**   The Organization has evaluated subsequent events through March 5, 2017, which is the date the financial statements were available to be issued. There were no events that required adjustments to or disclosures in the financial statements.

Example 2A

The United States Charity

Supplemental Information

> The auditor chose to issue the opinion on supplemental information separately instead of as an additional paragraph in their opinion on the financial statements.

Example 2A

The United States Charity

Independent Auditor's Report on Supplemental Information

To the Board of Directors
The United States Charity

Our audits of the financial statements included in the preceding section of this report were conducted for the purpose of forming an opinion on those statements as a whole. The supplemental information presented in the following section of this report is presented for purposes of additional analysis and is not a required part of the financial statements. Such information is the responsibility of management and was derived from and relates directly to the underlying accounting and other records used to prepare the financial statements. The information has been subjected to the auditing procedures applied in the audits of the financial statements and certain additional procedures, including comparing and reconciling such information directly to the underlying accounting and other records used to prepare the financial statements or to the financial statements themselves, and other procedures in accordance with auditing standards generally accepted in the United States of America. In our opinion, the information is fairly stated in all material respects in relation to the financial statements as a whole.

March 5, 2017

Example 2A

The United States Charity

Schedule of Functional Expenses

For the year ended December 31, 2016

	Program Services			Supporting Services			
	Information Dissemination	Research	Total Program Services	General and Administrative	Fundraising	Total Supporting Services	Total
Consulting fees	$ 2,084,998	$ -	$ 2,084,998	$ 68,898	$ 291,525	$ 360,423	$ 2,445,421
Professional fees	3,372	235,264	238,636	448,248	-	448,248	686,884
Salaries and benefits	430,029	24,175	454,204	400,316	272,387	672,703	1,126,907
Communications and public relations	136,749	-	136,749	-	-	-	136,749
Travel	62,090	1,752	63,842	10,604	71,538	82,142	145,984
Occupancy	-	-	-	233,920	-	233,920	233,920
Office supplies and small equipment	669	-	669	14,743	1,573	16,316	16,985
Telecommunications and web hosting	5,483	-	5,483	37,954	1,698	39,652	45,135
Meetings	20,523	-	20,523	741	1,033	1,774	22,297
Miscellaneous	18,197	-	18,197	17,392	12,883	30,275	48,472
Insurance	-	-	-	2,225	-	2,225	2,225
Depreciation and amortization	-	-	-	13,036	-	13,036	13,036
Equipment rental and maintenance	-	-	-	2,031	300	2,331	2,331
Interest expense	-	-	-	781	-	781	781
Allocation of shared expenses	104,610	13,378	117,988	(148,520)	30,532	(117,988)	-
Total expenses	$ 2,866,720	$ 274,569	$ 3,141,289	$ 1,102,369	$ 683,469	$ 1,785,838	$ 4,927,127

Example 2A

The United States Charity

Schedule of Functional Expenses

For the period from inception through December 31, 2015

	Program Services			Supporting Services			
	Information Dissemination	Research	Total Program Services	General and Administrative	Fundraising	Total Supporting Services	Total
Consulting fees	$ 559,590	$ -	$ 559,590	$ 250,207	$ 3,883	$ 254,090	$ 813,680
Professional fees	176,780	197,709	374,489	118,408	-	118,408	492,897
Salaries and benefits	133,051	-	133,051	143,748	-	143,748	276,799
Communications and public relations	132,096	-	132,096	11,681	-	11,681	143,777
Travel	59,080	-	59,080	138	76	214	59,294
Occupancy	-	-	-	255,900	-	255,900	255,900
Office supplies and small equipment	-	-	-	26,036	-	26,036	26,036
Telecommunications and web hosting	1,664	14	1,678	20,208	72	20,280	21,958
Meetings	9,296	-	9,296	465	-	465	9,761
Miscellaneous	17	-	17	9,109	-	9,109	9,126
Insurance	-	-	-	6,045	-	6,045	6,045
Depreciation and amortization	-	-	-	2,930	-	2,930	2,930
Equipment rental and maintenance	-	-	-	1,849	-	1,849	1,849
Allocation of shared expenses	131,184	-	131,184	(131,184)	-	(131,184)	-
Total expenses	$ 1,202,758	$ 197,723	$ 1,400,481	$ 715,540	$ 4,031	$ 719,571	$ 2,120,052

Exercise 2A: Working with Financial Statements

Use the financial statements in Example 2A for The United States Charity to familiarize yourself with a basic nonprofit financial statement.

1. Begin by looking at the independent auditor's report:
   a. What type of opinion is this?

   _____

   _____

   b. What period is covered by the report?

   _____

   _____

2. Locate the (1) Statements of Financial Position, (2) Statements of Activities, and (3) Statements of Cash Flows:
   a. How much are total assets on December 31, 2016?

   _____

   _____

   b. How much cash (and cash equivalents) did the organization have on December 31, 2016? Which two statements can you use to obtain this information?

   _____

   _____

   c. How much are total liabilities on December 31, 2016?

   _____

   _____

   d. How much are total unrestricted net assets on December 31, 2016?

   _____

   _____

   e. How much are total temporarily restricted net assets on December 31, 2016?

   _____

   _____

   f. What is the organization's change in net assets (bottom line) for FY 2016?

   _____

   _____

3. Focusing on the Statements of Financial Position:
   a. What does the statement tell you about the organization's financial position as of December 31, 2016?

   _____

   _____

   b. Has the organization's liquidity improved or declined from the period ended December 31, 2015 to FY 2016?

   _____

   _____

   c. What new assets exist in FY 2016?

   _____

   _____

   d. Do you expect the organization to pay its bills when they come due?

   _____

   _____

   e. What are the organization's largest liabilities at December 31, 2016?

   _____

   _____

   f. What new liabilities has the organization incurred in FY 2016?

   _____

   _____

4. Moving to the Statements of Activities:
   a. How does the total change in net assets for FY 2016 compare to the total change in net assets for the period that ended on December 31, 2015?

   _____

   _____

   b. What is this decrease attributable to?

   _____

   _____

   c. What are the key sources of revenue?

   _____

   _____

   d. Which program service is the organization's largest?

_____

_____

5. On to the Statements of Cash Flows:
   a. What method of presentation did the organization use for this statement?

_____

_____

   b. Did the amount of cash and cash equivalents increase or decrease during FY 2016? By how much?

_____

_____

   c. Which section of the statement would you look to for information on purchases of fixed assets? Did the organization spend more or less cash on purchases of fixed assets in FY 2016 than in the period that ended on December 31, 2015?

_____

_____

   d. Which section of the statement would you look to for information on purchases of investments? Did the organization spend more or less cash on purchases of investments in FY 2016 than in the period that ended on December 31, 2015?

_____

_____

   e. How did the investments fare in the current economy? Where did you find this information?

_____

_____

   f. Why are the lease obligation and the asset capitalized under the capital lease not shown in the main part of the statement?

_____

_____

6. And do not forget the footnotes:
   a. Where can you find information regarding all the significant accounting policies used by the organization?

_____

_____

b. Where can you find information that discusses management's plans related to the current decline in revenue and the decrease in net assets?

_____

_____

c. What use are the FY 2016 temporarily restricted net assets designated for? Where did you find this information?

_____

_____

7. And finally, examine the Supplemental Information:
   a. What is the title of the supplemental schedule?

_____

_____

   b. What are the total professional fees in FY 2016? Where did you find this information?

_____

_____

   c. What was the total expense related to the Information Dissemination program in FY 2016? Which two statements can you obtain this information from?

_____

_____

8. Among the most important issues revealed by the financial statements are the following:

_____

_____

Exercise 2A: Answers

1. Begin by looking at the independent auditor's report:
   a. What type of opinion is this?
      Unmodified.

   b. What period is covered by the report?
      The year ending December 31, 2016, and the period from inception (June 15, 2015) through December 31, 2015.

2. Locate the (1) Statements of Financial Position, (2) the Statements of Activities, and (3) the Statements of Cash Flows:
   a. How much are total assets on December 31, 2016?
      $2,755,165.

   b. How much cash (and cash equivalents) did the organization have on December 31, 2016? Which two statements can you use to obtain this information?
      $765,827. Statements of Financial Position and Statements of Cash Flows.

   c. How much are total liabilities on December 31, 2016?
      $748,068.

   d. How much are total unrestricted net assets on December 31, 2016?
      $257,097.

   e. How much are total temporarily restricted net assets on December 31, 2016?
      $1,750,000.

   f. What is the organization's change in net assets (bottom line) for FY 2016?
      $(595,438).

3. Focusing on the Statements of Financial Position:
   a. What does the statement tell you about the organization's financial position as of December 31, 2016?
      This statement tells you, among other things, that the organization's assets exceed its liabilities, and that its net assets have declined in FY 2016.

   b. Has the organization's liquidity improved or declined from the period ended December 31, 2015 to FY 2016?
      The organization's liquidity has declined from 2015 to 2016 since the organization has less cash available to satisfy their liabilities, which have increased.

   c. What new assets exist in FY 2016?
      Prepaid expenses and investments.

   d. Do you expect the organization to pay its bills when they come due?
      Yes. The organization currently has sufficient cash to meet its liabilities.

e. What are the organization's largest liabilities at December 31, 2016?

Accounts payable and accrued expenses of $606,228.

f. What new liabilities has the organization incurred in FY 2016?

Capital lease payable and deferred rent liability.

4. Moving to the Statements of Activities:

a. How does the total change in nets assets for FY 2016 compare to the total change in net assets for the period that ended on December 31, 2015?

There has been a large decrease in the change in net assets between these dates. The period that ended on December 31, 2015, had a positive change in net assets of $2,602,535, and the year that ended December 31, 2016, had a negative change in net assets of $(595,438).

b. What is this decrease attributable to?

The organization has experienced a decline in grants and contributions overall (need to consider the total of unrestricted and temporarily restricted grants and contributions), and expenses have increased sharply even as revenue has decreased.

c. What are the key sources of revenue?

Grants and contributions.

d. Which program service is the organization's largest?

Information dissemination.

5. On to the Statements of Cash Flows:

a. What method of presentation did the organization use for this statement?

Indirect method.

b. Did the amount of cash and cash equivalents increase or decrease during FY 2016? By how much?

Decreased by $(1,281,937).

c. Which section of the statement would you look to for information on purchases of fixed assets? Did the organization spend more or less cash on purchases of fixed assets in FY 2016 than in the period that ended on December 31, 2015?

Cash flows from investing activities section. Less was spent in FY 2016. The organization spent $13,373 during the year that ended on December 31, 2016, and $33,725 in the period that ended on December 31, 2015.

d. Which section of the statement would you look to for information on purchases of investments? Did the organization spend more or less cash on purchases of investments in FY 2016 than in the period that ended on December 31, 2015?

Cash flows from investing activities section. The organization spent more in FY 2016. The organization spent $35,000 for the year that ended on December 31, 2016, and none for the period that ended on December 31, 2015.

e. How did the investments fare in the current economy? Where did you find this information?

There was an unrealized loss of $(10,000) per the adjustment section under Operating Activities in the Statements of Cash Flows and in Note 3.

f. Why are the lease obligation and the asset capitalized under the capital lease not shown in the main part of the statement?

This is a noncash transaction since debt was exchanged for the assets. No cash was involved, so this is disclosed in the supplemental cash flow information that can be presented on the statement or in the footnotes.

6. And do not forget the footnotes:
   a. Where can you find information regarding all the significant accounting policies used by the organization?

   Note 1—Organization and Summary of Significant Accounting Policies.

   b. Where can you find information that discusses management's plans related to the current decline in revenue and the decrease in net assets?

   Note 12.

   c. What use are the FY 2016 temporarily restricted net assets designated for? Where do you find this information?

   They are for general operations. They are only time restricted for 2017 per Note 4.

7. And finally, examine the Supplemental Information:
   a. What is the title of the supplemental schedule?

   Schedule of Functional Expenses.

   b. What are the total professional fees in FY 2016? Where did you find this information?

   $686,884. Supplemental Schedule of Functional Expenses.

   c. What was the total expense related to the Information Dissemination program in FY 2016? Which two statements can you obtain this information from?

   $2,866,720. This can be found in both the Statements of Activities and the Supplemental Schedule of Functional Expenses.

8. Among the most important issues revealed by the financial statements are the following:
   - *This statement is a challenge to analyze, not only because the periods of operation differ but also because The United States Charity receives both unrestricted and temporarily restricted revenue.*
   - *As mentioned earlier in the materials, temporarily restricted revenue and expenses must be accounted for separately in the Statements of Activities. In this statement, a "layered" approach is used: unrestricted revenue and expenses are reported on initially, leading to a change in unrestricted net assets. Then temporarily restricted income is reported, with a resulting change in temporarily restricted net assets. The two changes in net assets are then summarized for a change in net assets for the organization as a whole.*

- *It is important to remember when reading this statement that accounting principles generally accepted in the United States of America (U.S. GAAP) requires that all expenses be treated as having been distributed from unrestricted net assets. To make this work, the temporarily restricted net assets that have been expended are released from the portion of the statement dealing with temporarily restricted net assets, thus reducing temporarily restricted net assets. They are simultaneously added to the revenue section of the unrestricted net assets.*

- *All of this aside, what of importance has happened? The best place to start is to look at the total change in net assets, which is the third line up from the bottom of the Statements of Activities. In the 2015 short fiscal year, the organization had a positive $2.6M increase in net assets, while in the full 2016 fiscal year, the organization lost $(595K). Clearly, things went seriously wrong and the board and management need to be very attentive.*

- *If we look at key revenue sources and expenses, the mathematics is fairly straightforward: unrestricted grants and contributions are up approximately $400K, while temporarily restricted grants and contributions are actually down by approximately $(550K). This is a net reduction of $(150K). Meanwhile, fundraising costs went from $4K to $683K, an enormous increase. This critical source of revenue had apparently been easily found at the start of the charity's existence, but became critically more difficult to acquire in its first full year of operations.*

- *As this was going on, the organization went about substantially increasing its programs and substantially increasing its general and administrative services for the full year that ended on December 31, 2016 ($1.7M and $387K, respectively). By reviewing the additional information provided in the Supplemental Schedules of Functional Expenses, it is possible to determine consultant fees more than tripled (from $814K to $2.4M) and that salary and benefits nearly quadrupled (from $277K to $1.1M). If the organization is to survive, these costs must be brought under control.*

- *The net result of all of this on the organization as a whole was a change from the 2015 short fiscal year positive change in net assets of $2.6M to a FY 2016 loss of $(595K). In Note 12, management has noted that they are addressing the issue of the decline in net assets and outline the steps they are taking to secure future funding and reductions in expenses for FY 2017 and beyond.*

- *The precipitous decline affected the Statements of Financial Position in a number of ways. Most obviously, the cash position dropped by well over half ($2M to $765K), taking an excellent liquidity situation at the end of the short 2015 fiscal period and making it considerably weaker at the end of FY 2016. Overall, total assets dropped by $(327K), while liabilities increased $268K.*

- *The Statements of Cash Flows also provides some absolutely critical information for the organization. For a young organization, having cash provided by operations is always excellent. In the short year that ended on December 31, 2015, operations added more than $2M—a very positive sign. Unfortunately, for the full year that ended on December 31, 2016, operations consumed more than $1.2M. It is information like this that can make the Statements of Cash Flows useful to review.*

Example 2B

The United States Charity

After Adoption of ASU 2016-14

Financial Statements

For the year ended December 31, 2016 and the period from inception (June 15, 2015) through December 31, 2015

Example 2B

The United States Charity

Independent Auditor's Report

To the Board of Directors
The United States Charity

Report on the Financial Statements

We have audited the accompanying statements of **The United States Charity** (the Organization), which comprise the statements of financial position as of December 31, 2016 and 2015, and the related statements of activities and cash flows for the year ended December 31, 2016 and the period from inception (June 15, 2015) through December 31, 2015, and the related notes to the financial statements.

Management's Responsibility for the Financial Statements

Management is responsible for the preparation and fair presentation of these financial statements in accordance with accounting principles generally accepted in the United States of America; this includes the design, implementation, and maintenance of internal control relevant to the preparation and fair presentation of financial statements that are free from material misstatement, whether due to fraud or error.

Auditor's Responsibility

Our responsibility is to express an opinion on these financial statements based on our audits. We conducted our audits in accordance with auditing standards generally accepted in the United States of America. Those standards require that we plan and perform the audit to obtain reasonable assurance about whether the financial statements are free from material misstatement.

An audit involves performing procedures to obtain audit evidence about the amounts and disclosures in the financial statements. The procedures selected depend on the auditor's judgment, including the assessment of the risks of material misstatement of the financial statements, whether due to fraud or error. In making those risk assessments, the auditor considers internal control relevant to the entity's preparation and fair presentation of the financial statements in order to design audit procedures that are appropriate in the circumstances, but not for the purpose of expressing an opinion on the effectiveness of the entity's internal control. Accordingly, we express no such opinion. An audit also includes evaluating the appropriateness of accounting policies used and the reasonableness of significant accounting estimates made by management, as well as evaluating the overall presentation of the financial statements.

We believe that the audit evidence we have obtained is sufficient and appropriate to provide a basis for our audit opinion.

Example 2B

The United States Charity

Opinion

In our opinion, the financial statements referred to above present fairly, in all material respects, the financial position of **The United States Charity** as of December 31, 2016 and 2015, and the changes in its net assets and its cash flows for the year ended December 31, 2016 and for the period from inception (June 15, 2015) through December 31, 2015, in accordance with accounting principles generally accepted in the United States of America.

March 5, 2017

Example 2B

This statement of financial position is not presented in a classified format.

The United States Charity

Statements of Financial Position

December 31,	2016	2015
Assets		
Cash and cash equivalents	$ 765,827	$ 2,047,764
Grants and contributions receivable	1,750,679	1,000,000
Prepaid expenses	20,178	-
Fixed assets, net of accumulated depreciation and amortization	163,102	28,614
Investments	25,000	-
Deposits	30,379	6,000
Total assets	$ 2,755,165	$ 3,082,378
Liabilities and Net Assets		
Accounts payable and accrued expenses	$ 606,228	$ 479,843
Capital lease payable	131,620	-
Deferred rent liability	10,220	-
Total liabilities	748,068	479,843
Commitments and contingencies		
Net assets		
Without donor restrictions	257,097	300,175
With donor restrictions	1,750,000	2,302,360
Total net assets	2,007,097	2,602,535
Total liabilities and net assets	$ 2,755,165	$ 3,082,378

The accompanying notes are an integral part of these financial statements.

Shaded lines indicate the basic totals that must be presented.

Example 2B

This is the layered format
for presenting net assets
by type.

The United States Charity

Statements of Activities

For the year ended December 31, 2016/period from inception through December 31, 2015	2016	2015
Changes in Net Assets without Donor Restrictions		
Revenue and support		
Grants and contributions	$ 2,560,000	$ 2,166,262
Investment return, net	21,548	30,653
Other income	141	223,312
Net assets released from restrictions due to expiration of time restrictions	2,302,360	-
Total revenue and support	4,884,049	2,420,227
Expenses		
Program services		
Information dissemination	2,866,720	1,202,758
Research	274,569	197,723
Total program services	3,141,289	1,400,481
Supporting services		
General and administrative	1,102,369	715,540
Fundraising	683,469	4,031
Total supporting services	1,785,838	719,571
Total expenses	4,927,127	2,120,052
Change in net assets without donor restrictions	(43,078)	300,175
Changes in Net Assets with Donor Restrictions		
Grants and contributions	1,750,000	2,302,360
Net assets released from time restrictions	(2,302,360)	-
Change in net assets with donor restrictions	(552,360)	2,302,360
Change in net assets	(595,438)	2,602,535
Net assets, beginning of year/inception	2,602,535	-
Net assets, end of year/period	$ 2,007,097	$ 2,602,535

The accompanying notes are an integral part of these financial statements.

This entity has not
elected the option to
categorize any items
as nonoperating.

Direct
method of
presentation.

Example 2B

The United States Charity

Statements of Cash Flows

For the year ended December 31, 2016/period from
inception through December 31, 2015

	2016	2015
Cash flows from operating activities		
Cash received from grantors and contributors	$ 2,559,321	$ 3,468,622
Cash collected on promises to give	999,321	-
Cash paid to employees	(1,821,262)	(367,091)
Cash paid to providers	(2,989,321)	(1,079,118)
Interest and dividends received	21,548	30,653
Other receipts	141	28,423
Interest paid	(781)	-
Net cash (used in) provided by operating activities	(1,231,033)	2,081,489
Cash flows from investing activities		
Purchases of investments	(35,000)	-
Purchases of fixed assets	(13,373)	(33,725)
Net cash used in investing activities	(48,373)	(33,725)
Cash flows from financing activities		
Payments on capital lease	(2,531)	-
Net cash used in financing activities	(2,531)	-
(Decrease) increase in cash and cash equivalents	(1,281,937)	2,047,764
Cash and cash equivalents, beginning of year/inception	2,047,764	-
Cash and cash equivalents, end of year/period	$ 765,827	$ 2,047,764
Supplemental cash flow information:		
Noncash financing activities:		
Leased property under capital lease	$ 134,151	$ -

The accompanying notes are an integral part of these financial statements.

Example 2B

The United States Charity

Notes to Financial Statements

1. Organization and Summary of Significant Accounting Policies

Organization

The United States Charity (the Organization) was incorporated on June 15, 2015 under the laws of the District of Columbia as a nonprofit organization. The Organization's goal is to be the nation's sole source of guidance for fundraising professionals. The Organization's activities are funded primarily through grants and contributions from foundations and corporations.

Basis of Accounting

The Organization's financial statements are presented in conformity with accounting principles generally accepted in the United States of America (U.S. GAAP) and have been prepared on the accrual basis of accounting.

Cash and Cash Equivalents

The Organization considers all deposits in banks to be cash equivalents. The cash and cash equivalents of the Organization are composed of amounts in accounts at banks.

Concentration of Credit Risk

The cash and cash equivalents of the Organization are composed of amounts in accounts at banks. While the amounts at times exceed the amount guaranteed by federal agencies and therefore bear some risk, the Organization has not experienced any loss of funds. As of December 31, 2016 and 2015, the amount in excess of the amount guaranteed by federal agencies was $469,666 and $2,080,459, respectively.

Fixed Assets

Furniture and equipment are stated at cost and are depreciated on a straight-line basis over the estimated useful lives of the respective assets, which range from three to five years. Leasehold improvements are amortized over the lesser of the estimated useful life of the asset or the remaining lease term. The asset and liability under the capital lease are recorded at the lower of the present value of the minimum lease payments or the fair value of the asset. The capital lease assets are amortized over the lower of the related lease term or their estimated useful life. Amortization of assets under the capital lease is included in depreciation and amortization expense for 2016. Expenditures for major repairs and improvements are capitalized. Expenditures for minor repairs and maintenance costs are expensed when incurred. Upon retirement or disposal of assets, the accounts are relieved of the cost and accumulated depreciation and amortization, with any resulting gain or loss included in revenue or expense.

Example 2B

The United States Charity

Notes to Financial Statements

The Organization capitalizes all expenditures for furniture and equipment and leasehold improvements over $250.

Investments

During the year ended December 31, 2016 the Organization invested $35,000 in institutional commingled funds that have no readily determinable market value and are valued at fair value as estimated by the fund. Because of the inherent uncertainty of valuation, it is reasonably possible that estimated values may differ from values that would have been used had a ready market for the securities existed. In addition, the fund may have risk associated with its concentrations in one geographic region and in certain industries.

Classification of Net Assets

The net assets of the Organization are reported as follows:

• Net assets without donor restrictions represent the portion of expendable funds that are available for support of the Organization's operations.

• Net assets with donor restrictions are specifically restricted by donors for various programs or future periods.

Revenue Recognition

Grants and contributions are reported as revenue in the year in which payments are received and/or unconditional promises are made. The Organization reports gifts of cash and other assets that are received with donor stipulations limiting the use of the donated assets as support without donor restrictions if all such donor restrictions are met in the year the award is received. Gifts of cash and other assets that are received with donor stipulations limiting the use of the donated assets are reported as net assets with donor restrictions if such donor stipulations are not fully met in the year the award is received. When a stipulated time restriction ends or purpose restriction is accomplished, net assets with donor restrictions are reclassified to net assets without donor restrictions and reported in the statements of activities as net assets released from restrictions.

Example 2B

The United States Charity

Notes to Financial Statements

Expenses

Expenses are recognized by the Organization on an accrual basis. Expenses paid in advance and not yet incurred are recorded as prepaid until the applicable period.

Liquidity and Availability

The Organization manages its liquid resources by focusing on fundraising efforts to ensure the entity has adequate contributions and grants to cover the programs that are being conducted. The Organization prepares very detailed budgets and has been very active in cutting costs to ensure the entity remains liquid.

As discussed in Note 10, the Organization maintains a line-of-credit to assist in meeting cash needs if they experience a lag between the receipt of contributions and grants and the payment of costs. This is a last resort option and the Organization did not have to use the line-of-credit during the year ended December 31, 2016 and the period from inception to December 31, 2015.

The following reflects the Organization's financial assets as of December 31, 2016 expected to be available within one year to meet the cash needs for general expenditures.

Cash and cash equivalents	$ 765,827
Grants and contributions receivable	1,750,679
	$ 2,516,506

The investments were not deemed to be available due to the nature of the investment and the lack of liquidity. The grants and contributions receivable are subject to implied time restrictions but are expected to be collected within one year.

Example 2B

The United States Charity

Notes to Financial Statements

Estimates

The preparation of financial statements in conformity with accounting principles generally accepted in the United States of America requires management to make estimates and assumptions that affect the reported amounts of assets and liabilities, disclosure of contingent assets and liabilities at the date of the financial statements, and the reported amounts of revenues and expenses during the reporting period. Accordingly, actual results could differ from those estimates.

Functional Allocation of Expenses

The costs of providing the various programs and other activities have been summarized on a functional basis in the accompanying statements of activities. Accordingly, certain costs have been allocated among the programs and supporting services benefited.

The Organization charges direct expenses incurred for a specific function directly to the program or supporting service category. These costs are those that can be identified as being incurred specifically for the activities of that program or supporting service. Other costs that are incurred for the Organization as a whole and benefit more than one program or supporting service are allocated on a reasonable basis that is consistently applied. The expenses that are allocated include occupancy, depreciation and amortization, and interest, which are allocated on a square-footage basis as well as salaries and benefits, which are allocated on the basis of estimates of time and effort. These are reflected in Note 12 in the line titled "Allocation of Shared Expenses." The Organization reevaluates its allocation method each year to determine if there are adjustments that are necessary to the allocation method based on actual activities conducted during the year.

Recent Accounting Pronouncement Adopted

The Society adopted the Financial Accounting Standards Board (FASB) Accounting Standards Update (ASU) 2016-14, "Not-for-Profit Entities (Topic 958): Presentation of Financial Statements of Not-for-Profit Entities" for fiscal year ended December 31, 2016. The adoption of this ASU had no effect on net assets as of December 31, 2016 and 2015 or the change in net assets presented for the year ended December 31, 2016 or the period from inception through December 31, 2015.

Example 2B

The United States Charity

Notes to Financial Statements

Recent Accounting Pronouncements to be Adopted

In May 2014, the FASB issued ASU 2014-09, "Revenue from Contracts with Customers (Topic 606)," which is a comprehensive new revenue recognition standard that will supersede existing revenue recognition guidance. The core principle of the guidance is that an entity should recognize revenue to depict the transfer of promised goods or services to customers in an amount that reflects the consideration to which the entity expects to be entitled in exchange for those goods or services. FASB issued ASU 2015-14 that deferred the effective date until annual periods beginning after December 15, 2018. Earlier adoption is permitted subject to certain limitations. The amendments in this update are required to be applied retrospectively to each prior reporting period presented or with the cumulative effect being recognized at the date of initial application. Management is currently evaluating the impact of this ASU on its financial statements.

In February 2016, the FASB issued ASU 2016-02, "Leases (Topic 842)," to increase transparency and comparability among organizations by recognizing lease assets and lease liabilities on the statement of financial position and disclosing key information about leasing arrangements for lessees and lessors. The new standard applies a right-of-use (ROU) model that requires, for all leases with a lease term of more than 12 months, an asset representing its right to use the underlying asset for the lease term and a liability to make lease payments to be recorded. The ASU is effective for fiscal years beginning after December 15, 2019 with early adoption permitted. Management is currently evaluating the impact of this ASU on its financial statements.

2. Grants and Contributions Receivable

Grants and contributions receivable of $1,750,679 and $1,000,000 at December 31, 2016 and 2015, respectively, includes grants and contributions from foundations for general support in the coming years. All contributions are due to be received within one year and are considered fully collectible.

3. Fair Value Measurements

The investment in commingled funds is stated at fair value of $25,000 based on the value as estimated by the fund manager and evaluated by management at December 31, 2016. Investment return consists of interest income of $31,548 and an unrealized loss on the commingled funds of $10,000. There were no external investment fees incurred related to this investment. Internal direct investment expenses were immaterial and are thus not netted against the investment return.

Example 2B

The United States Charity

Notes to Financial Statements

The Organization follows U.S. GAAP which establishes a common definition for fair value to be applied under generally accepted accounting principles requiring use of fair value, establishes a framework for measuring fair value, and expands disclosures about such fair value measurements.

U.S. GAAP defines fair value as the price that would be received to sell an asset or paid to transfer a liability (i.e., the "exit price") in an orderly transaction between market participants at the measurement date. Measurement date is the date of the financial statements. U.S. GAAP establishes a hierarchy for inputs used in measuring fair value that maximizes the use of observable inputs and minimizes the use of unobservable inputs by requiring that observable inputs be used when available.

Observable inputs are inputs that market participants would use in pricing the asset or liability developed based on market data obtained from sources independent of the Organization. Unobservable inputs are inputs that reflect the Organization's estimates about the assumptions market participants would use in pricing the asset or liability developed based on the best information available under the circumstances.

The hierarchy is broken down into three levels based on the reliability of the inputs as follows:

Level 1: Valuation based on quoted market prices in active markets for identical assets or liabilities. Since valuations are based on quoted prices that are readily and regularly available in an active market, valuation of these products does not entail a significant degree of judgment.

Level 2: Valuation based on quoted market prices of investments that are not actively traded or for which certain significant inputs are not observable, either directly or indirectly.

Level 3: Valuation based on inputs that are unobservable and significant to the overall fair value measurement.

All of the Organization's assets are classified as Level 3 in the fair value hierarchy.

Example 2B

The United States Charity

Notes to Financial Statements

The following table sets forth a summary of the changes in the fair value of the Organization's level 3 assets for the year ended December 31, 2016:

Level 3 Assets:

Balance, beginning of year	$	-
Purchases		35,000
Unrealized loss		(10,000)
Balance, end of year	$	25,000

4. Net Assets with Donor Restrictions

Net assets with donor restrictions of $1,750,000 and $2,302,360 as of December 31, 2016 and 2015, respectively, are for general operations but designated by third-party donors for use during the years ending December 31, 2017 and 2016, respectively, so they are subject only to time restrictions.

5. Contributed Services

During the year ended December 31, 2016 there were no contributed services and materials. During the period from inception through December 31, 2015, the Organization received donated services totaling $223,312 representing the fair value of these goods and services. Such donations included $11,312 of donated consulting fees and $12,000 of donated professional services and $200,000 of donated office space. Donated contributions have been recorded as other income in the accompanying statements of activities. Donated consulting and professional fees are included in general and administrative expense in the accompanying statements of activities. The donated office space expense was allocated among the programs and supporting services benefited based on square footage.

6. Income Taxes

Under Section 501(c)(3) of the Internal Revenue Code, the Organization is exempt from federal taxes on income other than net unrelated business income. For the year ended December 31, 2016 and the period from inception through December 31, 2015, no provision for income taxes was made as the Organization had no net unrelated business income.

Management believes it has no material uncertain tax positions or any related penalties and interest to accrue for the year ended December 31, 2016 and the period from inception through December 31, 2015. The Organization is still open to examination by taxing authorities from 2015 forward.

Example 2B

The United States Charity

Notes to Financial Statements

7. Fixed Assets

The following is a summary of fixed assets at December 31:

Year/period ended December 31,	2016	2015
Furniture and equipment	$ 38,537	$ 31,416
Leased property under capital lease	134,151	-
Leasehold improvements	6,252	-
Subtotal	178,940	31,416
Less allowance for depreciation and amortization	(15,838)	(2,802)
Fixed assets, net	$ 163,102	$ 28,614

Depreciation and amortization expense for the year ended December 31, 2016 and the period from inception through December 31, 2015 were $13,036 and $2,930, respectively.

8. Capital Lease

The Organization has entered into a master lease agreement with a financial institution to finance certain office equipment, furniture, and leasehold improvement additions. Under the terms of the master lease agreement there are two separate schedules that provide for the repayment of the amounts financed over the life of the assets purchased that expire in 2019 and 2021. The master lease agreement is secured by the assets purchased.

Example 2B

The United States Charity

Notes to Financial Statements

The following is an analysis of the leased property under the capital lease by major classes:

Asset balances at December 31, 2016		
Classes of property:		
Furniture and equipment	$	118,330
Leasehold improvements		15,821
Subtotal		134,151
Less accumulated amortization		(2,895)
Total	$	131,256

Minimum future lease payments under the capital lease master agreement as of December 31, 2016 through expiration are:

Years ending December 31,		
2017	$	39,751
2018		39,751
2019		37,920
2020		17,780
2021		16,299
Total minimum lease payments		151,501
Less amount representing interest		(19,881)
Present value of net minimum lease payments	$	131,620

The interest rate on the master lease is 7%, and is imputed based on the lower of the Organization's incremental borrowing rate at the inception of the leases or the lessor's implicit rate of return.

9. Lease Commitment In January 2016, the Organization entered into a lease for office space. The lease term commenced on January 1, 2016 and will expire on January 31, 2020. The lease provides for scheduled annual rent increases of 3%. In accordance with U.S. GAAP rent expense is recorded monthly on a straight-line basis in the amount of $19,493. This resulted in a deferred rent liability as of December 31, 2016 in the amount of $10,220. Rental expense for the year ended December 31, 2016 was $233,920.

Example 2B

The United States Charity

Notes to Financial Statements

The future minimum lease payments under this lease on an annual basis are as follows:

Years ending December 31,

2017	$ 240,940
2018	248,169
2019	255,614
2020	21,886
Total	$ 766,609

10. Line-of-Credit

On December 15, 2015, the Organization entered into a line-of-credit, not to exceed $100,000. This line-of-credit bears interest at the Wall Street Journal prime rate of interest plus 1.5 percentage points, which was 4.75% at December 31, 2016 and 4.5% at December 31, 2015. The line-of-credit is secured by substantially all the assets of the Organization and contains restrictive financial covenants such as the use of proceeds, financial information, other debts and liens. As of December 31, 2016 and 2015, the Organization did not have an outstanding balance due on the line-of-credit.

11. Description of Program and Supporting Services

Information Dissemination

The Organization regularly monitors the activities of fundraising professionals to find ways to improve results and improve campaigns. This information is disseminated through various channels.

Research

The Organization works to compile high-quality measures and data that can be used to assess the progress of charity work throughout the nation.

General and Administrative

This supporting service category includes the functions necessary to secure proper administrative functioning of the Organization's governing board, maintain an adequate working environment, and manage financial responsibilities of the Organization.

Fundraising

This supporting service category includes expenditures which provide the structure necessary to encourage and secure private financial support. No fundraising cost are allocated to programs or supporting services.

Entity chose to present the required analysis of expenses by function and nature in the footnotes based on the options included in ASU 2016-14.

Example 2B

The United States Charity

Notes to Financial Statements

12. Functional Expenses   The tables below present expenses by both their function and nature for the year ended December 31, 2016 and the period from inception through December 31, 2015.

For the year ended December 31, 2016

	Program Services			Supporting Services			
	Information Dissemination	Research	Total Program Services	General and Administrative	Fundraising	Total Supporting Services	Total
Consulting fees	$ 2,084,998	$ -	$ 2,084,998	$ 68,898	$ 291,525	$ 360,423	$ 2,445,421
Professional fees	3,372	235,264	238,636	448,248	-	448,248	686,884
Salaries and benefits	430,029	24,175	454,204	400,316	272,387	672,703	1,126,907
Communications and public relations	136,749	-	136,749	-	-	-	136,749
Travel	62,090	1,752	63,842	10,604	71,538	82,142	145,984
Occupancy	-	-	-	233,920	-	233,920	233,920
Office supplies and small equipment	669	-	669	14,743	1,573	16,316	16,985
Telecommunications and web hosting	5,483	-	5,483	37,954	1,698	39,652	45,135
Meetings	20,523	-	20,523	741	1,033	1,774	22,297
Miscellaneous	18,197	-	18,197	17,392	12,883	30,275	48,472
Insurance	-	-	-	2,225	-	2,225	2,225
Depreciation and amortization	-	-	-	13,036	-	13,036	13,036
Equipment rental and maintenance	-	-	-	2,031	300	2,331	2,331
Interest expense	-	-	-	781	-	781	781
Allocation of shared expenses	104,610	13,378	117,988	(148,520)	30,532	(117,988)	-
Total expenses	$ 2,866,720	$ 274,569	$ 3,141,289	$ 1,102,369	$ 683,469	$ 1,785,838	$ 4,927,127

For the period from inception through December 31, 2015

	Program Services			Supporting Services			
	Information Dissemination	Research	Total Program Services	General and Administrative	Fundraising	Total Supporting Services	Total
Consulting fees	$ 559,590	$ -	$ 559,590	$ 250,207	$ 3,883	$ 254,090	$ 813,680
Professional fees	176,780	197,709	374,489	118,408	-	118,408	492,897
Salaries and benefits	133,051	-	133,051	143,748	-	143,748	276,799
Communications and public relations	132,096	-	132,096	11,681	-	11,681	143,777
Travel	59,080	-	59,080	138	76	214	59,294
Occupancy	-	-	-	255,900	-	255,900	255,900
Office supplies and small equipment	-	-	-	26,036	-	26,036	26,036
Telecommunications and web hosting	1,664	14	1,678	20,208	72	20,280	21,958
Meetings	9,296	-	9,296	465	-	465	9,761
Miscellaneous	17	-	17	9,109	-	9,109	9,126
Insurance	-	-	-	6,045	-	6,045	6,045
Depreciation and amortization	-	-	-	2,930	-	2,930	2,930
Equipment rental and maintenance	-	-	-	1,849	-	1,849	1,849
Allocation of shared expenses	131,184	-	131,184	(131,184)	-	(131,184)	-
Total expenses	$ 1,202,758	$ 197,723	$ 1,400,481	$ 715,540	$ 4,031	$ 719,571	$ 2,120,052

Example 2B

The United States Charity

Notes to Financial Statements

13. Management's Plans   During the year ended December 31, 2016 the Organization had a decrease in net assets of approximately $595,000. Even with net assets available for use in 2017 of over $2 million, the Organization is acting to secure future funding, to carefully control and configure expenses, make programmatic progress and continue as a going concern.

Aggressive and diversified fundraising efforts are being pursued to increase contributed income during 2017 and beyond. Reduced expenditures are reflected in the 2017 budget going forward. As of the report date, the grants and contributions receivable shown in the December 31, 2016 statements of financial position, as well as new funding, have been received and cash balances are in excess of $2.1 million.

14. Subsequent Events   The Organization has evaluated subsequent events through March 5, 2017, which is the date the financial statements were available to be issued. There were no events that required adjustments to or disclosures in these financial statements.

Exercise 2B: Working with Financial Statements

Use the financial statements in Example 2B for The United States Charity to familiarize yourself with a basic nonprofit financial statement.

1. Begin by looking at the independent auditor's report:
   a. What type of opinion is this?

   _____

   _____

   b. What period is covered by the report?

   _____

   _____

2. Locate the (1) Statements of Financial Position, (2) Statements of Activities, and (3) Statements of Cash Flows:
   a. How much are total assets on December 31, 2016?

   _____

   _____

   b. How much cash (and cash equivalents) did the organization have on December 31, 2016? Which two statements can you use to obtain this information?

   _____

   _____

   c. How much are total liabilities on December 31, 2016?

   _____

   _____

   d. How much are total net assets without donor restrictions on December 31, 2016?

   _____

   _____

   e. How much are total net assets with donor restrictions on December 31, 2016?

   _____

   _____

   f. What is the organization's change in net assets (bottom line) for FY 2016?

   _____

   _____

3. Focusing on the Statements of Financial Position:

   a. What does the statement tell you about the organization's financial position as of December 31, 2016?

   _____

   _____

   b. Has the organization's liquidity improved or declined from the period that ended on December 31, 2015 to FY 2016?

   _____

   _____

   c. What new assets exist in FY 2016?

   _____

   _____

   d. Do you expect the organization to pay its bills when they come due?

   _____

   _____

   e. What are the organization's largest liabilities on December 31, 2016?

   _____

   _____

   f. What new liabilities has the organization incurred in FY 2016?

   _____

   _____

4. Moving to the Statements of Activities:

   a. How does the total change in net assets for FY 2016 compare to the total change in net assets for the period that ended on December 31, 2015?

   _____

   _____

   b. What is this decrease attributable to?

   _____

   _____

   c. What are the key sources of revenue?

   _____

   _____

   d. Which program service is the organization's largest?

_____

_____

5. On to the Statements of Cash Flows:
   a. What method of presentation did the organization use for this statement?

_____

_____

   b. Which section of the statement would you look to for information on purchases of fixed assets? Did the organization spend more or less cash on purchases of fixed assets in FY 2016 than in the period that ended on December 31, 2015?

_____

_____

   c. Which section of the statement would you look to for information on purchases of investments? Did the organization spend more or less cash on purchases of investments in FY 2016 than in the period that ended on December 31, 2015?

_____

_____

   d. Why are the lease obligation and the asset capitalized under the capital lease not shown in the main part of the statement?

_____

_____

6. And do not forget the footnotes:
   a. Where can you find information regarding all the significant accounting policies used by the organization?

_____

_____

   b. Where can you find information that discusses management's plans related to the current decline in revenue and the decrease in net assets?

_____

_____

   c. What use are the FY 2016 net assets with donor restrictions designated for? Where did you find this information?

_____

_____

    d. What are the total professional fees in FY 2016?

    _____

    _____

    e. What was the total expense related to the Information Dissemination program in FY 2016?

    _____

    _____

7. Which components of the financial statements reflect the adoption of ASU 2016-14?

    _____

    _____

8. Among the most important issues revealed by the financial statements are the following:

    _____

    _____

Exercise 2B: Answers

1. Begin by looking at the auditor's report:
    a. What type of opinion is this?
    Unmodified.

    b. What period is covered by the report?
    The year ending December 31, 2016, and the period from inception (June 15, 2015) through December 31, 2015.

2. Locate the (1) Statements of Financial Position, (2) the Statements of Activities, and (3) the Statements of Cash Flows:
    a. How much are total assets on December 31, 2016?
    $2,755,165.

    b. How much cash (and cash equivalents) did the organization have on December 31, 2016? Which two statements can you use to obtain this information?
    $765,827. Statements of Financial Position and Statements of Cash Flows.

    c. How much are total liabilities on December 31, 2016?
    $748,068.

    d. How much are total net assets without donor restrictions on December 31, 2016?
    $257,097.

    e. How much are total net assets with donor restrictions on December 31, 2016?
    $1,750,000.

    f. What is the organization's change in net assets (bottom line) for FY 2016?
    $(595,438).

3. Focusing on the Statements of Financial Position:
    a. What does the statement tell you about the organization's financial position as of December 31, 2016?

    This statement tells you, among other things, that the organization's assets exceed its liabilities, and that its net assets have declined in FY 2016.

    b. Has the organization's liquidity improved or declined from the period that ended on December 31, 2015 to FY 2016?

    The organization's liquidity has declined from 2015 to 2016 since the organization has less cash available to satisfy its liabilities, which have increased.

    c. What new assets exist in FY 2016?
    Prepaid expenses and investments.

    d. Do you expect the organization to pay its bills when they come due?
    Yes. The organization currently has sufficient cash to meet its liabilities.

e. What are the organization's largest liabilities?

Accounts payable and accrued expenses of $606,228.

f. What new liabilities has the organization incurred in FY 2016?

Capital lease payable and deferred rent liability.

4. Moving to the Statements of Activities:

a. How does the total change in net assets for FY 2016 compare to the total change in net assets for the period that ended on December 31, 2015?

There has been a large decrease in the change in net assets between these dates. The period that ended on December 31, 2015, had a positive change in net assets of $2,602,535, and the year that ended December 31, 2016, had a negative change in net assets of $(595,438).

b. What is this decrease attributable to?

The organization has experienced a decline in grants and contributions overall (need to consider the total of contributions without donor restrictions and contributions with donor restrictions), and expenses have increased sharply even as revenue has decreased.

c. What are the key sources of revenue?

Grants and contributions.

d. Which program service is the organization's largest?

Information dissemination.

5. On to the Statements of Cash Flows:

a. What method of presentation did the organization use for this statement?

Direct method.

b. Which section of the statement would you look to for information on purchases of fixed assets? Did the organization spend more or less cash on purchases of fixed assets in FY 2016 than in the period that ended on December 31, 2015?

Cash flows from investing activities section. Less was spent in FY 2016. The organization spent $13,373 during the year that ended December 31, 2016, and $33,725 in the period that ended on December 31, 2015.

c. Which section of the statement would you look to for information on purchases of investments? Did the organization spend more or less cash on purchases of investments in FY 2016 than in the period that ended on December 31, 2015?

Cash flows from investing activities section. The organization spent more in FY 2016. The organization spent $35,000 for the year that ended on December 31, 2016, and none for the period that ended on December 31, 2015.

d. Why are the lease obligation and the asset capitalized under the capital lease not shown in the main part of the statement?

This is a noncash transaction since debt was exchanged for the assets. No cash was involved, so this is disclosed in the supplemental cash flow information that can be presented on the statement or in the footnotes.

6. And do not forget the footnotes:

   a. Where can you find information regarding all the significant accounting policies used by the organization?

   Note 1—Organization and Summary of Significant Accounting Policies.

   b. Where can you find information that discusses management's plans related to the current decline in revenue and the decrease in net assets?

   Note 13.

   c. What use are the FY 2016 net assets with donor restrictions designated for? Where do you find this information?

   They are for general operations. They are only time restricted for 2017 per Note 4.

   d. What are the total professional fees in FY 2016?

   $686,884.

   e. What was the total expense related to the Information Dissemination program in FY 2016?

   $2,866,720.

7. Which components of the financial statements reflect the adoption of ASU 2016-14?

   - *Change in terminology from unrestricted net assets to net assets without donor restrictions and from temporarily restricted net assets to net assets with donor restrictions.*
   - *Liquidity and Availability disclosures in Note 1, Organization and Summary of Significant Accounting Policies (the entity had already included this before the adoption but other entities may not have).*
   - *Functional allocation methodology for expenses is included in Note 1, Organization and Summary of Significant Accounting Policies.*
   - *The effect of adopting ASU 2016-14 is in Note 1, Organization and Summary of Significant Accounting Policies.*
   - *The required analysis of expenses by function and nature was included as Note 12.*

8. Among the most important issues revealed by the financial statements are the following:

   - *This statement is a challenge to analyze not only because the periods of operation differ but also because The United States Charity receives some income that is without donor restriction and some income that is with donor restriction.*
   - *As mentioned earlier in the materials, income and expenses that have donor restrictions must be accounted for separately on the Statements of Activities. In this statement, a "layered" approach is used: revenue and expenses without donor restriction are reported on initially, leading to a change in net assets without donor restrictions. Then income with donor restrictions is reported, with a resulting change in net assets with donor restrictions. The change in net assets without donor restrictions is combined with the change in net assets with donor restrictions for a final total change in net assets for the organization as a whole.*
   - *It is important to remember when reading this statement that accounting principles generally accepted in the United States of America (U.S. GAAP) requires that all expenses be treated as having been distributed from net assets without donor restrictions. To make this work, the net*

assets with donor restrictions that have been expended are released from the portion of the statement dealing with net assets with donor restrictions, thus reducing net assets with donor restrictions. They are simultaneously added to the revenue section of the net revenue from activities without donor restrictions.

- *All of this aside, what of importance has happened? The best place to start is to look at the total change in net assets, which is the third line up from the bottom of the Statements of Activities. In the 2015 short fiscal year, the organization had a positive $2.6M increase in net assets, while in the full 2016 fiscal year, the organization lost $(595K). Clearly, things went seriously wrong and the board and management need to be very attentive.*

- *If we look at key revenue sources and expenses, the mathematics are fairly straightforward: grants and contributions without donor restrictions are up approximately $400K, while grants and contributions with donor restrictions are actually down by approximately $(550K). This is a net reduction of $(150K). Meanwhile, fundraising costs went from $4K to $683K, an enormous increase. This critical source of revenue had apparently been easily found at the start of the charity's existence, but became critically more difficult to acquire in its first full year of operations.*

- *As this was going on, the organization went about substantially increasing its programs and substantially increasing its general and administrative services for the full year that ended on December 31, 2016 ($1.7M and $387K, respectively). By reviewing the detail provided in Note 12 that shows the required analysis of expenses by function and nature, it is possible to determine consultant fees more than tripled (from $814K to $2.4M) and that salary and benefits nearly quadrupled (from $277K to $1.1M). If the organization is to survive, these costs must be brought under control.*

- *The net result of all of this on the organization as a whole was a change from the 2015 short fiscal year positive change in net assets of $2.6M to a FY 2016 loss of $(595K). In Note 13, management has noted that they are addressing the issue of the decline in net assets and outline the steps they are taking to secure future funding and reductions in expenses for FY 2017 and beyond.*

- *The precipitous decline affected the Statements of Financial Position in a number of ways. Most obviously, the cash position dropped by well over half ($2M to $765K), taking an excellent liquidity situation at the end of the short 2015 fiscal period and making it considerably weaker at the end of FY 2016. Overall, total assets dropped by $(327K), while liabilities increased $268K.*

- *The Statements of Cash Flows also provides some absolutely critical information for the organization. For a young organization, having cash provided by operations is always excellent. In the short year that ended on December 31, 2015, operations added more than $2M—a very positive sign. Unfortunately, for the full year that ended on December 31, 2016, operations consumed more than $1.2M. It is information like this that can make the Statements of Cash Flows useful to review.*

CHAPTER 20

Example Set 3

The following examples refer to an association named the Society of Analysts. The Society has a related foundation, the Society of Analysts Foundation, and presents consolidated financial statements. Collectively, the entity is referred to as the Organization. The Organization had a new auditor in fiscal year 2016 and only single-year financial statements are being presented based on an agreement between the Organization and its external auditor. Despite the lack of comparative information, much insight can still be gained from these statements as you will learn from reviewing the statements and answering the subsequent questions.

Example 3A: Prepared using accounting guidance before the adoption of ASU 2016-14.

Example 3B: Prepared after the adoption of ASU 2016-14.

Example 3A

Society of Analysts and Affiliate

Before the Adoption of ASU 2016-14

Consolidated Financial Statements

Year Ended December 31, 2016

Example 3A

Society of Analysts and Affiliate

Independent Auditor's Report

To the Board of Directors
Society of Analysts and Affiliate

Report on the Consolidated Financial Statements

We have audited the accompanying consolidated financial statements of the Society of Analysts and Affiliate (collectively referred to as the Organization), which comprise the consolidated statement of financial position as of December 31, 2016, and the related consolidated statementsof activitiesand cash flows for the year then ended, and the related notes to the consolidated financial statements.

Management's Responsibility for the Financial Statements

Management is responsible for the preparation and fair presentation of these consolidated financial statements in accordance with accounting principles generally accepted in the United States of America; this includes the design, implementation, and maintenance of internal control relevant to the preparation and fair presentation of consolidated financial statements that are free from material misstatement, whether due to fraud or error.

Auditor's Responsibility

Our responsibility is to express an opinion on these consolidated financial statements based on our audit. We conducted our audit in accordance with auditing standards generally accepted in the United States of America. Those standards require that we plan and perform the audit to obtain reasonable assurance about whether the consolidated financial statements are free from material misstatement.

An audit involves performing procedures to obtain audit evidence about the amounts and disclosures in the consolidated financial statements. The procedures selected depend on the auditor's judgment, including the assessment of the risks of material misstatement of the consolidated financial statements, whether due to fraud or error. In making those risk assessments, the auditor considers internal control relevant to the entity's preparation and fair presentation of the consolidated financial statements in order to design audit procedures that are appropriate in the circumstances, but not for the purpose of expressing an opinion on the effectiveness of the entity's internal control. Accordingly, we express no such opinion. An audit also includes evaluating the appropriateness of accounting policies used and the reasonableness of significant accounting estimates made by management, as well as evaluating the overall presentation of the consolidated financial statements.

We believe that the audit evidence we have obtained is sufficient and appropriate to provide a basis for our audit opinion.

Example 3A

Society of Analysts and Affiliate

Basis for Qualified Opinion

As described more fully in Note 17 to the consolidated financial statements, the Organization does not follow the accounting principles generally accepted in the United States of America that require recognition of the amount of contributed services as revenue and expenses in the consolidated financial statements. It was not practicable to determine the effects of the unrecorded contribution revenue and expenses on the consolidated financial statements.

Opinion

In our opinion, except for the effects of the matter described in the Basis for Qualified Opinion paragraph, the consolidated financial statements referred to above present fairly, in all material respects, the financial position of the Society of Analysts and Affiliateas of December 31, 2016, and the changes in their net assets and their cash flows for the year then ended in accordance with accountingprinciples generally accepted in the United States of America.

March 27, 2017

Example 3A

Society of Analysts and Affiliate

Consolidated Statement of Financial Position

December 31,	2016
Assets	
Current assets	
Cash and cash equivalents	$ 613,337
Accounts receivable—trade, net of allowance for uncollectible amounts of $4,351	81,234
Contributions receivable, net	79,645
Prepaid expenses	130,892
Total current assets	905,108
Noncurrent assets	
Investments, including Analyst Endowment	10,408,931
Property and equipment, net	418,170
Contributions receivable, net of current portion	42,047
Total noncurrent assets	10,869,148
Total assets	$ 11,774,256
Liabilities and Net Assets	
Current liabilities	
Line-of-credit	$ 475,000
Accounts payable and accrued expenses	810,200
Deferred revenue	1,496,130
Capital lease obligation	18,936
Total current liabilities	2,800,266
Noncurrent liabilities	
Capital lease obligation, net of current portion	6,917
Total noncurrent liabilities	6,917
Total liabilities	2,807,183
Commitments and contingencies	
Net assets	
Unrestricted	5,963,128
Temporarily restricted	592,312
Permanently restricted	2,411,633
Total net assets	8,967,073
Total liabilities and net assets	$ 11,774,256

See accompanying notes to consolidated financial statements.

Shaded lines indicate the basic totals that must be presented.

Example 3A

Society of Analysts and Affiliate

This example shows
the columnar
presentation.

Consolidated Statement of Activities

Year ended December 31, 2016

	Unrestricted	Temporarily Restricted	Permanently Restricted	Total
Revenue, Gains, and Other Support				
Membership dues	$ 5,719,729	$ -	$ -	$ 5,719,729
Education, meetings, and events	305,886	-	-	305,886
Conferences and courses	234,558	-	-	234,558
Contributions	1,864,366	-	200,000	2,064,366
Grants	1,198,854	-	-	1,198,854
Net assets released from restrictions:				
Satisfaction of time/program restrictions	184,168	(184,168)	-	-
Total operating revenue, gains, and other support	9,507,561	(184,168)	200,000	9,523,393
Expenses				
Program services				
Strategic marketing and communications	1,940,037	-	-	1,940,037
Research and knowledge resources	771,819	-	-	771,819
Customer service	287,456	-	-	287,456
Continuing education	1,516,370	-	-	1,516,370
Total program services	4,515,682	-	-	4,515,682
Supporting services				
Governance	352,519	-	-	352,519
Finance and administration	4,000,738	-	-	4,000,738
Fundraising	47,576	-	-	47,576
Total supporting services	4,400,833	-	-	4,400,833
Total operating expenses	8,916,515	-	-	8,916,515
Operating revenues in excess of operating expenses, before nonoperating	591,046	(184,168)	200,000	606,878
Nonoperating:				
Investment return, net	592,540	318,803	-	911,343
Total nonoperating activity	592,540	318,803	-	911,343
Change in net assets	1,183,586	134,635	200,000	1,518,221
Net assets, beginning of year	4,779,542	457,677	2,211,633	7,448,852
Net assets, end of year	$ 5,963,128	$ 592,312	$ 2,411,633	$ 8,967,073

See accompanying notes to consolidated financial statements.

Example 3A

Society of Analysts and Affiliate

Consolidated Statement of Cash Flows

Year Ended December 31,	2016
Cash flows from operating activities	
Change in net assets	$ 1,518,221
Adjustments to reconcile change in net assets to net cash provided by operating activities:	
Net realized and unrealized gains on investments	(473,478)
Depreciation and amortization	415,334
Permanently restricted contributions	(200,000)
(Increase) decrease in assets	
Accounts receivable—trade	52,805
Contributions receivable	111,950
Prepaid expenses	(40,563)
Increase (decrease) in liabilities	
Accounts payable and accrued expenses	247,398
Deferred revenue	11,363
Net cash provided by operating activities	1,643,030
Cash flows from investing activities	
Proceeds from sales of investments	10,241,892
Purchases of investments	(11,369,411)
Purchases of property and equipment	(132,027)
Proceeds from permanently restricted contributions for endowment	200,000
Net cash used in investing activities	(1,059,546)
Cash flows from financing activities	
Proceeds from line-of-credit	475,000
Payments on line-of-credit	(500,000)
Principal payments on capital lease obligation	(373,539)
Net cash used in financing activities	(398,539)
Increase in cash and cash equivalents	184,945
Cash and cash equivalents, beginning of year	428,392
Cash and cash equivalents, end of year	$ 613,337

Supplemental cash flow information:

Cash paid for interest	$ 12,614

See accompanying notes to consolidated financial statements.

Example 3A

Society of Analysts and Affiliate

Notes to Consolidated Financial Statements

1. Organizations

The Society of Analysts (the Society) is a national organization of analysts dedicated to reviewing the health of the nation's financial institutions.

The Society of Analysts Foundation (the Foundation) is a nonprofit organization, which establishes scholarships and grants, awarding them to deserving analysts. The Foundation is affiliated with the Society through common board members, therefore requiring consolidation with the financial statements of the Society.

2. Summary of Significant Accounting Policies

Principles of Consolidation

The consolidated financial statements include the accounts of the Society and the Foundation and are collectively referred to as the Organization. Inter-organizational accounts and transactions have been eliminated in consolidation.

Basis of Accounting

The consolidated financial statements of the Organization are presented in conformity with accounting principles generally accepted in the United States of America (U.S. GAAP) and have been prepared on the accrual basis of accounting.

Cash and Cash Equivalents

The Organization considers all highly liquid instruments, which are to be used for current operations and which have an original maturity of three months or less, to be cash and cash equivalents. All other highly liquid instruments, which are to be used for the long-term purposes of the Organization, are considered investments.

Accounts Receivable: Trade

This balance consists of amounts due to the Organization from members, training course application fees, and registrations.

Accounts receivable are stated at their net realizable value. The allowance method is used to determine uncollectible amounts. The allowance is based upon prior years' experience and management's analysis of subsequent collections. If actual collections experience changes, revisions to the allowance may be required. Accounts receivable are written off when deemed uncollectible.

As of December 31, 2016, the Organization believes that the allowance for uncollectible amounts is adequate. However, future write-offs may exceed the estimated allowance recorded.

Example 3A

Society of Analysts and Affiliate

Notes to Consolidated Financial Statements

Contributions Receivable

Unconditional promises to give that are expected to be collected within one year are recorded at net realizable value. Unconditional promises to give that are expected to be collected in future years are initially recorded at fair value using present value techniques incorporating risk-adjusted discount rates designed to reflect the assumptions market participants would use in pricing the asset. In subsequent years, amortization of the discounts is included in contributions revenue in the consolidated statement of activities.

The allowance method is used to determine the uncollectible amounts. The allowance is based upon prior years' experience and management's analysis of subsequent collections. Allowances on contributions receivable are recorded when circumstances indicate collection is doubtful for particular contributions receivable or as a general reserve for all contributions receivable. Contributions receivable are written off if reasonable collection efforts prove unsuccessful. Bad debt expense is reflected in fundraising expenses on the consolidated statement of activities when allowances on contributions receivable are increased or when contributions receivable written off exceed available allowances.

Conditional promises to give are not included as support until the conditions are substantially met.

Investments

Investments are recorded at readily determinable fair market values. Fair value is defined as the price that will be received to sell an asset or transfer a liability in an orderly transaction between market participants at the measurement date. Unrealized and realized gains and losses are included in the consolidated statement of activities.

Property and Equipment

Property and equipment are stated at cost, or at fair value, for contributed assets, and are depreciated and amortized over their estimated useful lives ranging from three to seven years. The straight-line method of depreciation and amortization is followed for all assets.

The Organization capitalizes all purchases of assets over $1,000 that have a useful life greater than one year. When assets are sold or disposed of, the cost and corresponding accumulated depreciation and amortization are removed from the accounts with any gain or loss reflected in current operations. Expenditures for repairs and maintenance are charged to expense as incurred.

Example 3A

Society of Analysts and Affiliate

Notes to Consolidated Financial Statements

Impairment of Long-Lived Assets

The Organization reviews asset carrying amounts whenever events or circumstances indicate that such carrying amounts may not be recoverable. When considered impaired, the carrying amount of the asset is reduced to its current fair value by a charge to the consolidated statement of activities. No indicators of impairment were identified for the year ended December 31, 2016.

Deferred Revenue

Deferred revenue consists of payments for memberships, grants, and conference revenue received in advance. Membership dues are recognized on a pro-rata basis over the annual membership period. The Organization recognizes grants and conference revenue when the related expenditures are incurred.

Unrestricted Net Assets

Unrestricted net assets consist of funds available for the general operations of the Organization.

The Organization's governing board has designated, as of December 31, 2016, $500,000 of net assets to establish a reserve for the future purchase of a building and $10,050 for a board-designated endowment.

Temporarily Restricted Net Assets

The Organization reports gifts of cash and other assets as restricted support if they are received with donor stipulations that limit the use of the donated assets. When a donor restriction expires, that is, when a stipulated time restriction ends or a purpose restriction is accomplished, temporarily restricted net assets are reclassified to unrestricted net assets and reported in the consolidated statement of activities as net assets released from restrictions.

Gains or losses on investments and other assets or liabilities are reported as increases or decreases in unrestricted net assets unless their use is restricted by explicit donor stipulation or by law.

Temporarily restricted net assets whose restrictions expire in the same year as receipt are classified as unrestricted revenue in the consolidated statement of activities.

Example 3A

Society of Analysts and Affiliate

Notes to Consolidated Financial Statements

<u>Permanently Restricted Net Assets</u>

Permanently restricted net assets consist of assets whose use by the Organization is limited by donor-imposed restrictions that neither expire by passage of time nor can be fulfilled or otherwise removed by actions of the Organization. The restrictions stipulate that resources be maintained permanently but permit the Organization to expend the income generated in accordance with the provisions of the agreements.

<u>Revenue Recognition</u>

Revenue is recognized during the period in which it is earned. Revenue received in advance and not yet earned is deferred to the applicable period. Contributions are reported when an unconditional promise to give is received.

<u>Expenses</u>

Expenses are recognized during the period in which they are incurred. Expenses paid in advance and not yet incurred are deferred to the applicable period.

<u>Functional Allocation of Expenses</u>

Entity chose to provide additional expense allocation information prior to adoption of ASU 2016-14.

The costs of providing various programs and supporting services are summarized on a functional basis in the consolidated statement of activities. Expenses are directly charged to the appropriate program activity, where feasible. Certain expenses, principally depreciation and amortization, rent, and insurance, have been allocated among the programs and supporting services based on a square-footage basis, as well as personnel costs, which are allocated based on the estimates of time and effort.

<u>Liquidity and Availability</u>

Entity chose to present this information prior to adoption of ASU 2016-14.

The following reflects the Organization's financial assets as of the consolidated statement of financial position date, reduced by amounts not available for general use because of contractual or donor-imposed restrictions within one year of the consolidated statement of financial position date. Amounts not available include amounts set aside for long-term investing in the endowment. However, amounts already appropriated from the donor-restricted endowment for general expenditure within one year of the consolidated statement of financial position date have not been subtracted as unavailable.

Example 3A

Society of Analysts and Affiliate

Notes to Consolidated Financial Statements

> Authors' Note:
> The financial assets used in calculating the starting point here are total assets, net of prepaid expenses and property and equipment, net. The $121,692 is the sum of current and long-term contributions receivable. The $2,882,253 is the sum of the temporarily restricted and permanently restricted net assets net of the total contributions receivable of $121,692.

Financial assets, at December 31, 2016	$ 11,225,194
Less those unavailable for general expenditures within one year, due to:	
Restricted by donor with time and purpose restrictions	(121,692)
Subject to appropriation and satisfaction of donor restrictions	(2,882,253)
Board designations:	
Amount designated for building	(500,000)
Board-designated endowment	(10,050)
Financial assets available to meet cash needs for general expenditures within one year	$ 7,711,199

The Organization manages its liquid resources by focusing on investing excess cash in investments that maximize earnings potential balanced with the amount of risk the Organization's Investment Committee has decided can be tolerated. The Organization receives a substantial portion of its revenue from membership dues, which are received largely in September of each year. To balance cash needs and meet financial obligations in a timely manner, the Organization uses a line-of-credit.

Measure of Operations

The Organization's operating revenues in excess of operating expenses include all operating revenues and expenses that are an integral part of its programs and supporting activities and net assets released from donor restrictions to support operating expenditures. The Organization has presented net investment return as nonoperating in the consolidated statement of activities.

Example 3A

Society of Analysts and Affiliate

Notes to Consolidated Financial Statements

<u>Use of Estimates</u>

The preparation of financial statements in conformity with accounting principles generally accepted in the United States of America (U.S. GAAP) requires management to make estimates and assumptions that affect certain reported amounts of assets and liabilities, disclosure of contingent assets and liabilities at the date of the consolidated financial statements, and the reported amounts of revenue and expenses during the reporting period. Actual results could differ from those estimates.

<u>Cash and Cash Equivalents, Investments, and Receivables</u>

Financial instruments which potentially subject the Organization to concentrations of credit risk consist principally of cash and cash equivalents, investments, and receivables. Cash and investment accounts are maintained at creditworthy financial institutions which at times may exceed federally insured limits. By policy, investments are kept within limits designed to prevent risks caused by concentration. Credit risk with respect to accounts receivable and contributions receivable are generally limited due to the fact that the Organization deals with customers and donors over a wide geographic area and that the individual balances are small dollar amounts.

<u>Risk and Uncertainties</u>

Due to the level of uncertainty related to changes in interest rates, market volatility, and credit risk, it is at least reasonably possible that changes in these risks could materially affect the fair value of investments reported in the accompanying consolidated statement of financial position as of December 31, 2016. However, management of the Organization is of the belief that the diversification of the Organization's invested assets among various asset classes should mitigate the impact of dramatic change on any one class. Further, because the values of the Organization's individual investments have and will fluctuate in response to changing market conditions, the amount of losses that will be recognized in subsequent periods, if any, cannot be determined.

Example 3A

Society of Analysts and Affiliate

Notes to Consolidated Financial Statements

Recent Accounting Pronouncements to be Adopted

In May 2014, the Financial Accounting Standards Board (FASB) issued Accounting Standards Update (ASU)2014-09, "Revenue from Contracts with Customers (Topic 606)," which is a comprehensive new revenue recognition standard that will supersede existing revenue recognition guidance. The core principle of the guidance is that an entity should recognize revenue to depict the transfer of promised goods or services to customers in an amount that reflects the consideration to which the entity expects to be entitled in exchange for those goods or services. FASB issued ASU 2015-14 that deferred the effective date until annual periods beginning after December 15, 2018. Earlier adoption is permitted subject to certain limitations. The amendments in this update are required to be applied retrospectively to each prior reporting period presented or with the cumulative effect being recognized at the date of initial application. Management is currently evaluating the impact of this ASU on its financial statements

In February 2016, the FASB issued ASU 2016-02, "Leases (Topic 842)," to increase transparency and comparability among organizations by recognizing lease assets and lease liabilities on the statement of financial position and disclosing key information about leasing arrangements for lessees and lessors. The new standard applies a right-of-use (ROU) model that requires, for all leases with a lease term of more than 12 months, an asset representing its right to use the underlying asset for the lease term and a liability to make lease payments to be recorded. The ASU is effective for fiscal years beginning after December 15, 2019 with early adoption permitted. Management is currently evaluating the impact of this ASU on its financial statements.

Example 3A

Society of Analysts and Affiliate

Notes to Consolidated Financial Statements

In August 2016, FASB issued ASU 2016-14, "Not-for-Profit Entities (Topic 958): Presentation of Financial Statements of Not-for-Profit Entities." The ASU amends the current reporting model for nonprofit organizations and enhances their required disclosures. The major changes include: (a) requiring the presentation of only two classes of net assets now entitled "net assets without donor restrictions" and "net assets with donor restrictions," (b) modifying the presentation of underwater endowment funds and related disclosures, (c) requiring the use of the placed in service approach to recognize the expirations of restrictions on gifts used to acquire or construct long-lived assets absent explicit donor stipulations otherwise, (d) requiring that all nonprofits present an analysis of expenses by function and nature in either the statement of activities, a separate statement, or in the notes and disclose a summary of the allocation methods used to allocate costs, (e) requiring the disclosure of quantitative and qualitative information regarding liquidity and availability of resources, (f) presenting investment return net of external and direct internal investment expenses, and (g) modifying other financial statement reporting requirements and disclosures intended to increase the usefulness of nonprofit financial statements. The ASU is effective for the financial statements for fiscal years beginning after December 15, 2017. Early adoption is permitted. The provisions of the ASU must be applied on a retrospective basis for all years presented although certain optional practical expedients are available for periods prior to adoption. Management is currently evaluating the impact of this ASU on its financial statements.

3. Income Taxes — The Society has been granted tax-exempt status under Section 501(c)(6) of the Internal Revenue Code (IRC). The Society is required to report unrelated business income to the Internal Revenue Service. The Society had an insignificant amount of unrelated business income for the year ended December 31, 2016.

The Foundation has been granted tax-exempt status under Section 501(c)(3) of the IRC and has been classified as an organization that is not a private foundation under IRC Section 509(a). The Foundation had no unrelated business income for the year ended December 31, 2016.

Example 3A

Society of Analysts and Affiliate

Notes to Consolidated Financial Statements

Income tax benefits are recognized for income tax positions taken or expected to be taken in a tax return, only when it is determined that the income tax position will more likely than not be sustained upon examination by taxing authorities. The Organization has analyzed tax positions taken for filing with the Internal Revenue Service and all state jurisdictions where it operates. The Organization believes that income tax filing positions will be sustained upon examination and does not anticipate any adjustments that would result in a material adverse effect on the Organization's consolidated financial position, change in net assets, or cash flows. Accordingly, the Organization has not recorded any reserves, or related accruals for interest and penalties for uncertain income tax positions at December 31, 2016. The Organization is still open to examination by taxing authorities for fiscal year 2013 and forward.

4.　Contributions Receivable

The Foundation has a fundraising campaign to award scholarships to analysts for research projects.

Contributions receivable consists of unconditional promises to give as follows at:

December 31,	2016
Amounts receivable in:	
Less than one year	$ 79,645
One to five years	102,570
Total unconditional promises to give	182,215
Less: discount to net present value at rates ranging from 2.96% to 4.70%	(16,398)
Less: allowance for uncollectible contributions receivable	
Net unconditional promises to give	121,692
Less: current portion	(79,645)
Noncurrent portion	$ 42,047

Example 3A

Society of Analysts and Affiliate

Notes to Consolidated Financial Statements

5. Investment Return

The following schedule summarizes the net investment return:

For the year ended December 31,	2016
Investment and interest earnings	$ 570,465
Investment expenses	(132,600)
Realized gains	663,745
Unrealized loss	(190,267)
	$ 911,343

> The Society already allocated direct internal investment expenses prior to adoption of ASU 2016-14.

6. Fair Value Measurements

U.S. GAAP establishes a consistent framework for measuring fair value and expands disclosures for each major asset and liability category measured at fair value on either a recurring or nonrecurring basis. U.S. GAAP states that fair value is an exit price, representing the amount expected to be received to sell an asset, or paid to transfer a liability, in an orderly transaction between market participants. As such, fair value is a market-based measurement that should be determined based on assumptions that market participants would use in pricing an asset or liability. To increase consistency and comparability in fair value measurements and related disclosures, U.S. GAAP sets forth a three-tier hierarchy for the inputs used to measure fair value based on the degree to which such inputs are observable in the marketplace, as follows:

Level 1: Valuation based on quoted prices in active markets for identical assets or liabilities that a reporting entity has the ability to access at the measurement date, and where transactions occur with sufficient frequency and volume to provide pricing information on an ongoing basis.

Example 3A

Society of Analysts and Affiliate

Notes to Consolidated Financial Statements

Level 2: Valuation based on inputs other than quoted prices included within Level 1 that are observable for the asset or liability, either directly or indirectly. Inputs include quoted prices for similar assets or liabilities in active markets, quoted prices for identical or similar assets or liabilities in markets that are not active, that is markets in which there are few transactions, prices are not current, or prices vary substantially over time.

Level 3: Valuation based on inputs that are unobservable for an asset or liability and shall be used to measure fair value to the extent that observable inputs are not available, thereby allowing for situations in which there is little, if any, market activity for the asset or liability at the measurement date. This input therefore reflects the Organization's assumptions about what market participants would use in pricing the asset or liability developed based on the best information available in the circumstances.

The Organization's investments in marketable securities (money market funds, equity mutual funds, and fixed income funds) are reported at fair value, based on quoted market prices. The fair value of the Organization's investments in marketable securities is determined to be Level 1 as they are traded in active markets.

The following table sets forth by level within the fair value hierarchy the Organization's investment assets and liabilities at fair value as of December 31, 2016. As required by U.S. GAAP, assets and liabilities are classified in their entirety based on the lowest level of input that is significant to the fair value measurement. The following table presents the Organization's investments that are measured at fair value on a recurring basis.

Example 3A

Society of Analysts and Affiliate

Notes to Consolidated Financial Statements

Investment Assets at Fair Value
as of December 31, 2016

	Level 1	Level 2	Level 3	Total
Investments:				
Equity Mutual Funds:				
U.S.-Blended	$ 2,552,165	$ -	$ -	$ 2,552,165
International Equity	2,416,953	-	-	2,416,953
U.S.-Large Cap Value	1,140,287	-	-	1,140,287
U.S.-Small Cap Value	545,894	-	-	545,894
U.S.-Small Cap Growth	112,259	-	-	112,259
Fixed Income Funds:	3,508,606	-	-	3,508,606
Money Market Funds:	132,767	-	-	132,767
Total investments at fair value	$ 10,408,931	$ -	$ -	$ 10,408,931

7. Property and Equipment

Property and equipment consists of the following at:

December 31,	2016
Furniture and equipment	$ 57,745
Computer equipment and software	1,809,897
	1,867,642
Less accumulated depreciation and amortization	(1,449,472)
Property and equipment, net	$ 418,170

Depreciation and amortization expense for the year ended December 31, 2016 was $415,334.

Example 3A

Society of Analysts and Affiliate

Notes to Consolidated Financial Statements

8. Line-of-Credit

During 2009, the Organization obtained a $500,000 line-of-credit with a financial institution. The interest on the line-of-credit is calculated at a variable rate of 1.5% over the LIBOR Market Index Rate. The interest rate as of December 31, 2016 was 2.40%. There was $475,000 outstanding on the line-of-credit at December 31, 2016. Any outstanding principal and accrued interest is due on demand. The line-of-credit expires August 14, 2018.The agreement requires the Organization to comply with certain financial and non-financial covenants.

9. Capital Leases

The Organization leases computer equipment under three separate capital leases expiring in the year 2018. The asset and liability under the capital leases is recorded at the lower of the present value of the minimum lease payments or the fair value of the assets. The assets are amortized over the lower of their related lease term or their estimated useful lives.

Amortization of the assets under the capital leases is included in depreciation and amortization expense for 2016. Following is a summary of the computer equipment held under capital leases at:

December 31,	2016
Computer equipment	$ 91,168
Less: allowance for amortization	(65,315)
	$ 25,853

Future minimum lease payments, by year and in the aggregate, under the capital leases are as follows at:

Year Ending December 31,	
2017	$ 20,843
2018	7,024
	27,867
Less: amount representing interest	(2,014)
Present value of future minimum lease payments	25,853
Less: current portion	(18,936)
Noncurrent capital lease obligation	$ 6,917

Example 3A

Society of Analysts and Affiliate

Notes to Consolidated Financial Statements

10. Temporarily Restricted Net Assets

Temporarily restricted net assets at December 31, 2016, consist of the following:

Promises to give, the proceeds of which have been restricted for scholarships	$ 121,692
Unspent appreciation of Endowment Funds which must be appropriated for expenditure before use restricted by donors for:	
Continuing Education Program	389,808
Research	80,812
Subtotal	470,620
Total	$ 592,312

11. Permanently Restricted Net Assets

Permanently restricted net assets consist of the following at:

December 31,	2016
Analyst Endowment	
Continuing Education Program	$ 1,569,620
Research	842,013
	$ 2, 411,633

The earnings related to the investment of these funds is restricted for use in the continuing education program and research program and are included in temporarily restricted net assets.

12. Endowment

The Organization's endowment consists of the Analyst Endowment fund, which consists of approximately 20 individual funds established for a variety of purposes. The endowment includes both donor-restricted endowment funds and funds designated by the Board to function as an endowment. As required by U.S. GAAP net assets associated with endowment funds, including funds designated by the Board to function as endowments, are classified and reported based on the existence or absence of donor-imposed restrictions.

Example 3A

Society of Analysts and Affiliate

Notes to Consolidated Financial Statements

> Should indicate the name of the state when identifying the UPMIFA regulations in the footnote.

The Board of the Organization has interpreted the Uniform Prudent Management of Institutional Funds Act (UPMIFA) as requiring the preservation of the original gift amount of the donor-restricted endowment funds, absent explicit donor stipulations to the contrary. As a result of this interpretation, the Organization classifies as permanently restricted net assets (a) the original value of gifts donated to the permanent endowment, (b) the original value of subsequent gifts to the permanent endowment, and (c) accumulations to the permanent endowment made in accordance with the direction of the applicable donor gift instrument at the time the accumulation is added to the fund. The remaining portion of the donor-restricted endowment fund that is not classified in permanently restricted net assets is classified as temporarily restricted net assets until those amounts are appropriated for expenditure by the Organization in a manner consistent with the standard of prudence prescribed by UPMIFA. In accordance with UPMIFA, the Organization considers the following factors in making a determination to appropriate or accumulate donor-restricted endowment funds:

(1) The duration and preservation of the fund,
(2) The purposes of the Organization and the donor-restricted endowment fund,
(3) General economic conditions,
(4) The possible effect of inflation and deflation,
(5) The expected total return from income and the appreciation of investments,
(6) Other resources of the Organization, and
(7) The investment policies of the Organization.

Endowment Net Asset Composition

The following table represents the composition of the Organization's endowment by net asset class at December 31, 2016:

	Unrestricted	Temporarily Restricted	Permanently Restricted	Total
Board-designated endowment funds	$ 10,050	$ -	$ -	$ 10,050
Donor-restricted endowment funds	(200,620)	470,620	2,411,633	2,681,633
Total endowment funds	$ (190,570)	$ 470,620	$ 2,411,633	$ 2,691,683

Example 3A

Society of Analysts and Affiliate

Notes to Consolidated Financial Statements

Changes in Endowment Net Assets

The following table represents the changes in the endowment funds during the year ended:

December 31, 2016	Unrestricted	Temporarily Restricted	Permanently Restricted	Total
Endowment net assets, beginning of the year	$ (190,975)	$ 235,907	$ 2,211,633	$ 2,256,565
Investment return	105	318,803	-	318,908
Contributions	-	-	200,000	200,000
Transfer to create board-designated endowment funds	500	-	-	500
Amounts appropriated for expenses	(200)	(84,090)	-	(84,290)
Endowment net assets, end of year	$ (190,570)	$ 470,620	$ 2,411,633	$ 2,691,683

Authors' note: The $200,620 deficit in unrestricted endowment net assets represents the amounts by which the fair value of certain donor-restricted endowment funds were below the amount required to be retained permanently. The temporarily restricted endowment net assets represent income earned on the permanently restricted net assets that have not been appropriated by the Organization for expenditure to date. The amount shown in this footnote as permanently restricted net assets agrees to the total of permanently restricted net assets on the consolidated statement of financial position. The amounts shown in this footnote reflect only the endowment net assets and the classification of the components. Thus, the amounts shown in the footnote as unrestricted and temporarily restricted net assets do not appear in the consolidated statement of financial position as separate amounts. These amounts are included in the totals shown in the consolidated statement of financial position for these net asset classes.

Example 3A

Society of Analysts and Affiliate

Notes to Consolidated Financial Statements

Funds with Deficiencies

From time to time, the fair value of assets associated with individual donor-restricted endowment funds may fall below the level that the donor or UPMIFA requires the Organization to retain as a fund of perpetual duration. Deficiencies of this nature that are reported in unrestricted net assets were ($200,620) as of December 31, 2016. These deficiencies resulted from unfavorable market fluctuations that occurred shortly after the investment of new permanently restricted contributions and continued appropriation for certain programs that was deemed prudent by the Board.

Return Objectives and Risk Parameters

The Organization has adopted investment and spending policies for endowment assets that attempt to provide a predictable stream of funding to programs supported by its endowment while seeking to maintain the purchasing power of the endowment assets. Endowment assets include those assets of donor-restricted funds that the organization must hold in perpetuity or for a donor-specified period as well as board-designated funds. Under this policy, as approved by the Board, the endowment assets are invested in a manner that is intended to produce results that exceed the price and yield results of the S&P 500 index while assuming a moderate level of investment risk. The Organization expects its endowment funds, over time, to provide an average rate of return of approximately 8 percent annually. Actual returns in any given year may vary from this amount.

Strategies Employed for Achieving Objectives

To satisfy its long-term rate-of-return objectives, the Organization relies on a total return strategy in which investment returns are achieved through both capital appreciation (realized and unrealized) and current yield (interest and dividends). The Organization targets a diversified asset allocation that places a greater emphasis on equity-based investments to achieve its long-term return objectives within prudent risk constraints.

Example 3A

Society of Analysts and Affiliate

Notes to Consolidated Financial Statements

<u>Spending Policy and How the Investment Objectives Relate to Spending Policy</u>

The Organization has a policy of appropriating for distribution each year 5 percent of its endowment fund's average fair value over the prior 12 quarters through the calendar year-end preceding the fiscal year in which the distribution is planned. In establishing this policy, the Organization considered the long-term expected return on its endowment. Accordingly, over the long term, the Organization expects the current spending policy to allow its endowment to grow at an average of 3 percent annually.

13. Description of Program and Supporting Services

The following program and supporting services are included in the consolidated statement of activities:

<u>Strategic Marketing and Communications</u>

Includes expenses incurred to further the Organization members' analyst services to the general public through specific marketing and media relations tactics. Also includes expenses for communicating current professional news to major media publications and Organization members.

<u>Research and Knowledge Resources</u>

Includes the costs of creating the Organization's member magazine. Also includes managing content on the Organization's website, editorial support services, and research service and the Foundation scholarship program.

<u>Customer Service</u>

Responsible for assisting all members with any request or information via telephone, e-mail, or web.

<u>Continuing Education</u>

The Organization offers a wide range of continuing education opportunities and knowledge of new techniques, products, important issues, and business management. These programs include workshops, lectures, and expenses related to the production and sale of educational materials.

<u>Governance</u>

Expenses cover costs relating to the governance structure of the Organization.

Example 3A

Society of Analysts and Affiliate

Notes to Consolidated Financial Statements

Finance and Administration

Includes the functions necessary to maintain an adequate working environment and manage financial and budgetary responsibilities of the Organization.

Fundraising

Includes costs associated with the production of events, mailings, and general solicitations of funds for the Foundation.

14. Retirement Plan

The Organization maintains a 401(k) Profit Sharing Plan and Trust that covers substantially all full-time employees once they have reached age 21 and have completed six months of service. Under the terms of the plan, the Organization matches:

a. 100% of the participating employees' contribution up to 6% of the employees' salary; and

b. 50% of the participating employees' contribution for the next 2% of the employees' salary.

Contribution expense to the plan for the year ended December 31, 2016, was $113,882.

15. Commitments and Contingencies

Lease

The Organization leases space for its office under an operating lease that expires in December 2020. The lease includes certain pass-through occupancy expenses that are charged each year. The future minimum lease commitments under this lease, by year and in the aggregate, are as follows:

Year ending December 31,	
2017	$ 130,000
2018	130,000
2019	130,000
2020	130,000
	$ 520,000

Rent expense for the year ended December 31, 2016 was $145,000.

Example 3A

Society of Analysts and Affiliate

Notes to Consolidated Financial Statements

<u>Litigation</u>

The Organization is subject to legal proceedings, claims, and liabilities which arise in the ordinary course of business. In the opinion of management, the amount of the ultimate liability with respect to those actions will not materially affect the Organization's consolidated financial position or cash flows.

16. Related Party Transactions	The Society performs various administrative tasks for the Foundation. The Society also provides office space and pays certain expenses on behalf of the Foundation and charges the Foundation for its share. The time and related salary for three Society staff members working on the Foundation is allocated to the Foundation and paid for from the Foundation budget.
17. Departure from U.S. GAAP	The Organization does not follow the generally accepted accounting principles that require the recognition of the amount of contributed services as revenue and expenses in the consolidated financial statements. It was not practicable to determine the effects of the unrecorded contribution revenue and expenses on the consolidated financial statements.
18. Subsequent Events	The Organization has evaluated subsequent events through March 27, 2017, which is the date the consolidated financial statements were available to be issued.
	There were no events noted that required adjustment to or disclosure in these consolidated financial statements.

Exercise 3A: Working with Financial Statements

Use the Society of Analysts and Affiliate consolidated financial statements in Example 3A to familiarize yourself with some of the concepts unique to nonprofit organizations.

1. Begin by looking at the independent auditor's report:
   a. What type of opinion is this?

   _____

   _____

   b. What period is covered by the report?

   _____

   _____

2. Locate the consolidated Statement of Financial Position:
   a. Locate the current and noncurrent portions of contributions receivable. What footnote provides information on the components of contributions receivable? What is the net amount of contributions receivable?

   _____

   _____

   b. Locate noncurrent investments. Where can you find information on the types of investments held by the organization? What is the total amount of investments?

   _____

   _____

   c. What types of net assets does the organization have? What portion of net assets can be used to fund general operations?

   _____

   _____

   d. What is the total amount of unrestricted net assets?

   _____

   _____

   e. What is the current ratio (current assets/current liabilities) on December 31, 2016?

   _____

   _____

3. Locate the consolidated Statement of Activities:
   a. What is the total change in temporarily restricted net assets?

   _____

   _____

b. What amount of permanently restricted contributions was received during the year? What does "permanently restricted" mean?

_____

_____

c. What is the total amount of net assets released from restrictions? What does this mean?

_____

_____

d. Did the organization's total operating revenues exceed operating expenses before net investment return?

_____

_____

4. Moving to the consolidated Statement of Cash Flows:
   a. What were the total unrealized and realized losses on investments? In what two places can you find this information?

   _____

   _____

   b. What amount did the organization borrow on the line-of-credit during the year? In what section of the statement did you find this information?

   _____

   _____

   c. Did cash increase or decrease from FY 2015 to FY 2016?

   _____

   _____

5. Focusing on the footnotes:
   a. What does the organization consider a cash and cash equivalent?

   _____

   _____

   b. How does the organization value its investments? What footnotes can you get this information from?

   _____

   _____

   c. What is the organization's capitalization policy for property and equipment?

_____

_____

   d. What is the total amount of furniture and equipment the organization has? What note contains this information?

_____

_____

   e. What programs are the organization's permanently restricted net assets restricted to? In which note can this be found?

_____

_____

   f. Describe the Strategic Marketing and Communications program. What note can this be found in?

_____

_____

6. Among the most important issues revealed by the consolidated financial statements are the following:

_____

_____

Exercise 3A: Answers

1. Begin by looking at the independent auditor's report:
   a. What type of opinion is this?

   Modified as a result of a departure from generally accepted accounting principles.

   b. What period is covered by the report?

   Year ended December 31, 2016.

2. Locate the consolidated Statement of Financial Position:
   a. Locate the current and noncurrent portions of contributions receivable. What footnote provides information on the components of contributions receivable? What is the net amount of contributions receivable?

   Note 4; $121,692.

   b. Locate noncurrent investments. Where can you find information on the types of investments held by the organization? What is the total amount of investments?

   Notes 2, 5, and 6; $10,408,931.

   c. What types of net assets does the organization have? What portion of net assets can be used to fund general operations?

   Unrestricted, temporarily restricted, and permanently restricted; unrestricted.

   d. What is the total amount of unrestricted net assets?

   $5,963,128.

   e. What is the current ratio (current assets/current liabilities) on December 31, 2016?

   The current ratio is .32, which is calculated by dividing current assets by current liabilities (905,108/2,800,266) and is considered a weak current ratio.

3. Locate the consolidated Statement of Activities:
   a. What is the total change in temporarily restricted net assets?

   $134,635.

   b. What amount of permanently restricted contributions was received during the year? What does "permanently restricted" mean?

   $200,000. These funds must be held in perpetuity and investment income spent in accordance with the donor's intent per the permanently restricted net assets footnote in Note 2, the Summary of Accounting Policies and Note 11.

   c. What is the total amount of net assets released from restrictions? What does this mean?

   $184,168. These funds were spent in accordance with the donors' intention, or the time restriction has elapsed.

d. Did the organization's total operating revenues exceed operating expenses before net investment return?

Yes, by $606,878.

4. Moving to the consolidated Statement of Cash Flows:

a. What were the total unrealized and realized losses on investments? In what two places can you find this information?

$(473,478); Statement of Cash Flows and Note 5.

b. What amount did the organization borrow on the line-of-credit during the year? In what section of the statement did you find this information?

$475,000; cash flows from financing activities.

c. Did cash increase or decrease from FY 2015 to FY 2016?

Cash increased by $184,945.

5. Focusing on the footnotes:

a. What does the organization consider a cash and cash equivalent?

All highly liquid instruments with an original maturity of three months or less that are to be used for current operations, which excludes those held as part of the organization's long-term investments per Note 2, the Summary of Accounting Policies, under the Cash and Cash Equivalents heading.

b. How does the organization value its investments? What footnotes can you get this information from?

At fair value; Note 2, Summary of Accounting Policies, under Investments and Notes 5 and 6.

c. What is the organization's capitalization policy for property and equipment?

The organization capitalizes assets with an original cost of $1,000 or greater per Note 2 under the Property and Equipment heading.

d. What is the total amount of furniture and equipment that the organization has? What note contains this information?

$57,745; Note 7.

e. What programs are the organization's permanently restricted net assets restricted to? In which note can this be found?

Continuing Education Program and Research Program; Note 11.

f. Describe the Strategic Marketing and Communications program. What note can this be found in?

Specific marketing and media relations tactics are used to further the organization's members' analyst services to the general public; Note 13.

6. Among the most important issues revealed by the consolidated financial statements are the following:

- *There are several important insights that the consolidated financial statements provide even though they are not comparative.*

- *Based on a review of the consolidated Statement of Financial Position, you can note that current liabilities exceed the current assets by nearly triple. Although the organization holds mutual funds and other liquid investments in its portfolio, they would need to liquidate these assets if they needed cash for general operations. There may be losses that are realized if the assets needed to be liquidated in a down market. The organization may want to obtain professional investment advice on how to possibly structure some investments as liquid assets that may not have the potential for a loss if they needed to liquidate these quickly.*

- *Also, as noted in the consolidated Statement of Financial Position, the organization owes $475,000 on its line-of-credit. The line-of-credit is used to offset timing differences between when the cash is received and when amounts are due. The membership dues are paid based on a September 30 due date, so there are often times when cash is needed throughout the year to smooth this out. The organization is incurring interest expense on these borrowings and should analyze this cost in comparison to the potential to restructure the investments as noted earlier to try to smooth these fluctuations out at the lowest possible cost.*

- *What is clear from the consolidated Statement of Activities is that the organization's single largest source of revenue is membership dues. This comprises 60 percent of total revenue. The organization may want to consider plans to further diversify its revenue streams to protect against future declines that could occur from dues. You would need to look at prior year financial statements to see the full picture of the trend in dues revenue.*

- *Based on looking at the consolidated Statement of Activities, you can also see that finance and administration costs of $4,000,738 nearly equal the total program costs of $4,515,682. The organization is incurring an inordinate amount of overhead costs to run its operations. Further investigation needs to be performed on this anomaly.*

Example 3B

Society of Analysts and Affiliate

After Adoption of ASU 2016-14

Consolidated Financial Statements

Year Ended December 31, 2016

Example 3B

Society of Analysts and Affiliate

Independent Auditor's Report

To the Board of Directors
Society of Analysts and Affiliate

Report on the Consolidated Financial Statements

We have audited the accompanying consolidated financial statements of the **Society of Analysts and Affiliate** (collectively referred to as the Organization), which comprise the consolidated statement of financial position as of December 31, 2016, and the related consolidated statements of activities and cash flows for the year then ended, and the related notes to the consolidated financial statements.

Management's Responsibility for the Financial Statements

Management is responsible for the preparation and fair presentation of these consolidated financial statements in accordance with accounting principles generally accepted in the United States of America; this includes the design, implementation, and maintenance of internal control relevant to the preparation and fair presentation of consolidated financial statements that are free from material misstatement, whether due to fraud or error.

Auditor's Responsibility

Our responsibility is to express an opinion on these consolidated financial statements based on our audit. We conducted our audit in accordance with auditing standards generally accepted in the United States of America. Those standards require that we plan and perform the audit to obtain reasonable assurance about whether the consolidated financial statements are free from material misstatement.

An audit involves performing procedures to obtain audit evidence about the amounts and disclosures in the consolidated financial statements. The procedures selected depend on the auditor's judgment, including the assessment of the risks of material misstatement of the consolidated financial statements, whether due to fraud or error. In making those risk assessments, the auditor considers internal control relevant to the entity's preparation and fair presentation of the consolidated financial statements in order to design audit procedures that are appropriate in the circumstances, but not for the purpose of expressing an opinion on the effectiveness of the entity's internal control. Accordingly, we express no such opinion. An audit also includes evaluating the appropriateness of accounting policies used and the reasonableness of significant accounting estimates made by management, as well as evaluating the overall presentation of the consolidated financial statements.

We believe that the audit evidence we have obtained is sufficient and appropriate to provide a basis for our audit opinion.

Example 3B

Society of Analysts and Affiliate

Basis for Qualified Opinion

As described more fully in Note 17 to the consolidated financial statements, the Organization does not/follow the accounting principles generally accepted in the United States of America that require recognition of the amount of contributed services as revenue and expenses in the consolidated financial statements. It was not practicable to determine the effects of the unrecorded contribution revenue and expenses on the consolidated financial statements.

Opinion

In our opinion, except for the effects of the matter described in the Basis for Qualified Opinion paragraph, the consolidated financial statements referred to above present fairly, in all material respects, the financial position of the **Society of Analysts and Affiliate** as of December 31, 2016, and the changes in its net assets and its cash flows for the year then ended in accordance with accounting principles generally accepted in the United States of America.

Emphasis of Matter

As discussed in Note 2 to the consolidated financial statements, the Organization has elected to adopt the Financial Accounting Standards Board Accounting Standards Update 2016-14, *Not-for-Profit Entities (Topic 958): Presentation of Financial Statements of Non-for-Profit Entities.* Our opinion is not modified with respect to this matter.

March 27, 2017

Example 3B

Society of Analysts and Affiliate

Classified presentation.

Consolidated Statement of Financial Position

December 31,		2016
Assets		
Current assets		
Cash and cash equivalents	$	613,337
Accounts receivable—trade, net of allowance		
for uncollectible amounts of $4,351		81,234
Contributions receivable, net		79,645
Prepaid expenses		130,892
Total current assets		905,108
Noncurrent assets		
Investments, including Analyst Endowment		10,408,931
Property and equipment, net		418,170
Contributions receivable, net of current portion		42,047
Total noncurrent assets		10,869,148
Total assets		$ 11,774,256
Liabilities and Net Assets		
Current liabilities		
Line-of-credit	$	475,000
Accounts payable and accrued expenses		810,200
Deferred revenue		1,496,130
Capital lease obligation		18,936
Total current liabilities		2,800,266
Noncurrent liabilities		
Capital lease obligation, net of current portion		6,917
Total noncurrent liabilities		6,917
Total liabilities		2,807,183
Commitments and contingencies		
Net assets		
Without donor restrictions:		
Undesignated	$ 5,653,698	
Designated by the Board for building reserve	500,000	
Board-designated endowment funds	10,050	
Subtotal without donor restrictions		6,163,748
With donor restrictions:		
Purpose restricted and time restricted	$ 121,692	
Perpetual in nature	2,882,253	
Underwater endowments	(200,620)	
Subtotal with donor restrictions		2,803,325
Total net assets		8,967,073
Total liabilities and net assets		$ 11,774,256

The level of detail presented here is not required, however if not shown here, it must be included in the footnotes.

See accompanying notes to consolidated financial statements.

Shaded lines indicate the basic totals that must be presented.

Example 3B

Society of Analysts and Affiliate

This example shows the columnar presentation.

Consolidated Statement of Activities

Year ended December 31, 2016

	Without Donor Restrictions	With Donor Restrictions	Total
Revenue, Gains, and Other Support			
Membership dues	$ 5,719,729	$ -	$ 5,719,729
Education, meetings, and events	305,886	-	305,886
Conferences and courses	234,558	-	234,558
Contributions	1,864,366	200,000	2,064,366
Grants	1,198,854	-	1,198,854
Net assets released from restrictions:			
Investment return appropriated and released from donor-restricted endowment	84,090	(84,090)	-
Satisfaction of time/program restrictions	100,078	(100,078)	-
Total operating revenue, gains, and other support	9,507,561	15,832	9,523,393
Expenses			
Program services			
Strategic marketing and communications	1,940,037	-	1,940,037
Research and knowledge resources	771,819	-	771,819
Customer service	287,456	-	287,456
Continuing education	1,516,370	-	1,516,370
Total program services	4,515,682	-	4,515,682
Supporting services			
Governance	352,519	-	352,519
Finance and administration	4,000,738	-	4,000,738
Fundraising	47,576	-	47,576
Total supporting services	4,400,833	-	4,400,833
Total operating expenses	8,916,515	-	8,916,515
Operating revenues in excess of operating expenses, before nonoperating	591,046	15,832	606,878
Nonoperating:			
Investment return, net	592,540	318,803	911,343
Total nonoperating activity	592,540	318,803	911,343
Change in net assets	1,183,586	334,635	1,518,221
Net assets, beginning of year	4,980,162	2,468,690	7,448,852
Net assets, end of year	$ 6,163,748	$ 2,803,325	$ 8,967,073

See accompanying notes to consolidated financial statements.

Example 3B

Society of Analysts and Affiliate

Consolidated Statement of Functional Expenses

Year ended December 31, 2016

| | Program Services | | | | | Supporting Services | | | | Total |
	Strategic Marketing and Communications	Research and Knowledge Resources	Customer Service	Continuing Education	Total Program Services	Governance	Finance and Administration	Fundraising	Total Supporting Services	Total Expenses
Salaries and wages	$ 827,715	$ 249,850	$ 87,989	$ 771,729	$ 1,937,283	$ 148,978	$ 2,443,703	$ 27,002	$ 2,619,683	$ 4,556,966
Benefits and taxes	215,205	64,960	22,877	200,648	503,690	38,734	623,360	7,020	669,114	1,172,804
Meeting costs	158,106	-	-	-	158,106	17,425	10,900	-	28,325	186,431
Contractors	129,827	61,017	12,902	14,559	218,305	-	313,072	390	313,462	531,767
Occupancy	45,000	20,000	5,000	60,000	130,000	2,000	12,000	1,000	15,000	145,000
Legal	63,077	23,831	30,989	39,383	157,280	20,989	69,689	1,200	91,878	249,158
Insurance	160,709	89,078	24,987	159,183	433,957	39,289	118,110	2,300	159,699	593,656
Printing, replication, and mailing	98,960	39,090	20,001	77,806	235,857	20,389	63,936	980	85,305	321,162
Service charges	7,396	5,948	2,090	17,483	32,917	1,090	4,651	550	6,291	39,208
Office supplies	65,883	38,940	20,214	33,897	158,934	32,982	27,292	1,902	62,176	221,110
Telephone, tech, Internet, and communications	71,674	39,089	45,098	61,909	217,770	12,930	121,489	2,930	137,349	355,119
Depreciation and amortization	90,367	35,951	13,389	70,641	210,348	16,420	186,366	2,200	204,986	415,334
Other miscellaneous expenses	6,118	3,987	1,920	9,132	21,157	1,293	6,170	102	7,565	28,722
Foundation scholarships	-	100,078	-	-	100,078	-	-	-	-	100,078
Total operating expenses	$ 1,940,037	$ 771,819	$ 287,456	$ 1,516,370	$ 4,515,682	$ 352,519	$ 4,000,738	$ 47,576	$ 4,400,833	$ 8,916,515

See accompanying notes to consolidated financial statements.

> Entities must present the required analysis of expenses by function and nature in one location. This information may be presented in a separate basic financial statement, the statement of activities, or the notes. This example shows the choice to present as a separate basic financial statement. Presenting this required information as supplemental information does not meet the ASU requirement.

Example 3B

Society of Analysts and Affiliate

Direct method of presentation.

Consolidated Statement of Cash Flows

Year Ended December 31,	2016
Cash flows from operating activities	
Cash received from members for services	$ 7,028,482
Cash received from donors and grantors	2,899,348
Cash received on contributions receivable	42,180
Interest and dividends received	570,465
Cash paid to scholarship recipients	(100,078)
Cash paid to employees and retirees	(5,765,001)
Cash paid to suppliers and vendors	(3,019,752)
Cash paid for interest	(12,614)
Net cash provided by operating activities	1,643,030
Cash flows from investing activities	
Proceeds from sales of investments	10,241,892
Purchases of investments	(11,369,411)
Purchases of property and equipment	(132,027)
Collections of contributions restricted for investment in endowment	200,000
Net cash used in investing activities	(1,059,546)
Cash flows from financing activities	
Proceeds from line-of-credit	475,000
Payments on line-of-credit	(500,000)
Principal payments on capital lease obligation	(373,539)
Net cash used in financing activities	(398,539)
Increase in cash and cash equivalents	184,945
Cash and cash equivalents, beginning of year	428,392
Cash and cash equivalents, end of year	$ 613,337

See accompanying notes to consolidated financial statements.

Organization chose not to present the reconciliation of the change in net assets from operating activities as permitted under ASU 2016-14 when using the direct method of presentation.

Example 3B

Society of Analysts and Affiliate

Notes to Consolidated Financial Statements

1. Organizations

The Society of Analysts (the Society) is a national organization of analysts dedicated to reviewing the health of the nation's financial institutions.

The Society of Analysts Foundation(the Foundation) is a nonprofit organization, which establishes scholarships and grants, awarding them to deserving analysts. The Foundation is affiliated with the Society through common board members, therefore requiring consolidation with the financial statements of the Society.

2. Summary of Significant Accounting Policies

Principles of Consolidation

The consolidated financial statements include the accounts of the Society and the Foundation and are collectively referred to as the Organization. Interorganizational accounts and transactions have been eliminated in consolidation.

Basis of Accounting

The consolidated financial statements of the Organization are presented in conformity with accounting principles generally accepted in the United States of America (U.S. GAAP) and have been prepared on the accrual basis of accounting.

Cash and Cash Equivalents

The Organization considers all highly liquid instruments, which are to be used for current operations and which have an original maturity of three months or less, to be cash and cash equivalents. All other highly liquid instruments, which are to be used for the long-term purposes of the Organization, are considered investments.

Accounts Receivable: Trade

This balance consists of amounts due to the Organization from members, training course application fees, and registrations.

Accounts receivable are stated at their net realizable value. The allowance method is used to determine uncollectible amounts. The allowance is based upon prior years' experience and management's analysis of subsequent collections. If actual collections experience changes, revisions to the allowance may be required. Accounts receivable are written off when deemed uncollectible.

Example 3B

Society of Analysts and Affiliate

Notes to Consolidated Financial Statements

As of December 31, 2016, the Organization believes that the allowance for uncollectible amounts is adequate. However, future write-offs may exceed the estimated allowance recorded.

Contributions Receivable

Unconditional promises to give that are expected to be collected within one year are recorded at net realizable value. Unconditional promises to give that are expected to be collected in future years are initially recorded at fair value using present value techniques incorporating risk-adjusted discount rates designed to reflect the assumptions market participants would use in pricing the asset. In subsequent years, amortization of the discounts is included in contributions revenue in the consolidated statement of activities.

The allowance method is used to determine the uncollectible amounts. The allowance is based upon prior years' experience and management's analysis of subsequent collections. Allowances on contributions receivable are recorded when circumstances indicate collection is doubtful for particular contributions receivable or as a general reserve for all contributions receivable. Contributions receivable are written off if reasonable collection efforts prove unsuccessful. Bad debt expense is reflected in fundraising expenses on the consolidated statement of activities when allowances on contributions receivable are increased or when contributions receivable written off exceed available allowances.

Conditional promises to give are not included as support until the conditions are substantially met.

Investments

Investments are recorded at readily determinable fair market values. Fair value is defined as the price that will be received to sell an asset or transfer a liability in an orderly transaction between market participants at the measurement date. Net investment return/(loss) is reported in the consolidated statement of activities and consists of interest and dividend income, realized and unrealized capital gains and losses, less external and direct internal investment expenses.

Property and Equipment

Property and equipment are stated at cost, or at fair value, for contributed assets, and are depreciated and amortized over their estimated useful lives ranging from three to seven years. The straight-line method of depreciation and amortization is followed for all assets.

Example 3B

Society of Analysts and Affiliate

Notes to Consolidated Financial Statements

The Organization capitalizes all purchases of assets over $1,000 that have a useful life greater than one year. When assets are sold or disposed of, the cost and corresponding accumulated depreciation and amortization are removed from the accounts with any gain or loss reflected in current operations. Expenditures for repairs and maintenance are charged to expense as incurred.

Impairment of Long-Lived Assets

The Organization reviews asset carrying amounts whenever events or circumstances indicate that such carrying amounts may not be recoverable. When considered impaired, the carrying amount of the asset is reduced to its current fair value by a charge to the consolidated statement of activities. No indicators of impairment were identified for the year ended December 31, 2016.

Deferred Revenue

Deferred revenue consists of payments for memberships, grants, and conference revenue received in advance. Membership dues are recognized on a pro-rata basis over the annual membership period. The Organization recognizes grants and conference revenue when the related expenditures are incurred.

Net Assets

Net assets, revenues, gains, and losses are classified based on the existence or absence of donor or grantor-imposed restrictions. Accordingly, net assets and changes therein are classified and reported as follows:

Net Assets without Donor Restrictions

Net assets without donor restrictions consist of funds available for the general operations of the Organization.

Board-Designated Net Assets

The Organization's governing board has designated, from net assets without donor restrictions, as of December 31, 2016, $500,000 of net assets to establish a reserve for the future purchase of a building and $10,050 for a board-designated endowment.

Example 3B

Society of Analysts and Affiliate

Notes to Consolidated Financial Statements

Net Assets with Donor Restrictions

The Organization reports gifts of cash and other assets as restricted support if they are received with donor or grantor stipulations that limit the use of the donated assets. Some donor-imposed restrictions are temporary in nature, such as those that will be met by the passage of time or other events specified by the donor. Other donor-imposed restrictions are perpetual in nature, where the donor stipulates that resources be maintained in perpetuity. When a donor restriction expires, that is, when a stipulated time restriction ends or a purpose restriction is accomplished net assets are reclassified to net assets without donor restrictions and reported in the consolidated statement of activities as net assets released from restrictions.

Gains or losses on investments and other assets or liabilities are reported as increases or decreases in net assets without donor restrictions unless their use is restricted by explicit donor stipulation or by law.

Net assets with donor restrictions whose restrictions expire (that is, when a stipulated time restriction ends or purpose restriction is accomplished) in the same year as the revenue is recognized are classified as revenue without donor restrictions in the consolidated statement of activities.

Revenue Recognition

Revenue is recognized during the period in which it is earned. Revenue received in advance and not yet earned is deferred to the applicable period. Contributions are reported when an unconditional promise to give is received.

Expenses

Expenses are recognized during the period in which they are incurred. Expenses paid in advance and not yet incurred are deferred to the applicable period.

Functional Allocation of Expenses

The costs of providing various programs and supporting services are summarized on a functional basis in the consolidated statement of activities. Expenses are directly charged to the appropriate program activity, where feasible. The financial statements report certain categories of expenses that are attributable to more than one program or supporting function. Therefore, these expenses require allocation on a reasonable basis that is consistently applied. The expenses that are allocated include depreciation and amortization, rent, and insurance, which are allocated based on a square-footage basis, as well as personnel costs, which are allocated based on the estimates of time and effort.

Example 3B

Society of Analysts and Affiliate

Notes to Consolidated Financial Statements

<u>Liquidity and Availability</u>

The following reflects the Organization's financial assets as of the consolidated statement of financial position date, reduced by amounts not available for general use because of contractual or donor-imposed restrictions within one year of the consolidated statement of financial position date. Amounts not available include amounts set aside for long-term investing in the endowment. However, amounts already appropriated from the donor-restricted endowment for general expenditure within one year of the consolidated statement of financial position date have not been subtracted as unavailable.

> Authors' Note:
> The financial assets used in calculating the starting point here are total assets, net of prepaid expenses and property and equipment, net. The $121,692 is the sum of current and long-term contributions receivable. The $2,882,253 is the sum of the temporarily restricted and permanently restricted net assets net of the total contributions receivable of $121,692.

Financial assets, at December 31, 2016	$ 11,225,194
Less those unavailable for general expenditures within one year, due to:	
Restricted by donor with time and purpose restrictions	(121,692)
Subject to appropriation and satisfaction of donor restrictions	(2,882,253)
Board designations:	
Amount designated for building	(500,000)
Board-designated endowment	(10,050)
Financial assets available to meet cash needs for general expenditures within one year	$ 7,711,199

The Organization manages its liquid resources by focusing on investing excess cash in investments that maximize earnings potential balanced with the amount of risk the Organization's Investment Committee has decided can be tolerated. The Organization receives a substantial portion of its revenue from membership dues which are received largely in September of each year. To balance cash needs and meet financial obligations in a timely manner, the Organization uses a line-of-credit.

Example 3B

Society of Analysts and Affiliate

Notes to Consolidated Financial Statements

Measure of Operations

The Organization's operating revenues in excess of operating expenses include all operating revenues and expenses that are an integral part of its programs and supporting activities and net assets released from donor restrictions to support operating expenditures. The measure of operations includes support for operating activities from both net assets with donor restrictions and net assets without donor restrictions designated for long-term investment (the donor-restricted and quasi-endowment) according to the Organization's spending policy, which is detailed in Note 11. The measure of operations excludes investment return in excess of amounts made available for current support.

Use of Estimates

The preparation of financial statements in conformity with accounting principles generally accepted in the United States of America (U.S. GAAP) requires management to make estimates and assumptions that affect certain reported amounts of assets and liabilities, disclosure of contingent assets and liabilities at the date of the financial statements, and the reported amounts of revenue and expenses during the reporting period. Actual results could differ from those estimates.

Cash and Cash Equivalents, Investments, and Receivables

Financial instruments which potentially subject the Organization to concentrations of credit risk consist principally of cash and cash equivalents, investments, and receivables. Cash and investment accounts are maintained at creditworthy financial institutions, which at times may exceed federally insured limits. By policy, investments are kept within limits designed to prevent risks caused by concentration. Credit risk with respect to accounts receivable and contributions receivable are generally limited due to the fact that the Organization deals with customers and donors over a wide geographic area and that the individual balances are small dollar amounts.

Risk and Uncertainties

Due to the level of uncertainty related to changes in interest rates, market volatility, and credit risk, it is at least reasonably possible that changes in these risks could materially affect the fair value of investments reported in the accompanying consolidated statement of financial position as of December 31, 2016. However, management of the Organization is of the belief that the diversification of the Organization's invested assets among various asset classes should mitigate the impact of dramatic change on any one class. Further, because the values of the Organization's individual investments have and will fluctuate in response to changing market conditions, the amount of losses that will be recognized in subsequent periods, if any, cannot be determined.

Example 3B

Society of Analysts and Affiliate

Notes to Consolidated Financial Statements

Recent Accounting Pronouncement Adopted

The Organization adopted the Financial Accounting Standards Board (FASB) Accounting Standards Update (ASU) 2016-14,"Not-for-Profit Entities (Topic 958): Presentation of Financial Statements of Not-for-Profit Entities," for fiscal year ended December 31, 2016. Due to the adoption of ASU 2016-14, the Organization had underwater endowments with deficiencies of $200,620 as of December 31, 2015 that were previously recorded as net assets without donor restrictions. Upon adoption of the ASU, this amount was transferred to net assets with donor restrictions. The adoption of this ASU increased net assets without donor restrictions by $200,620 and decreased net assets with donor restrictions by this amount as of December 31, 2015. There was no effect on the change in net assets reported at December 31, 2016.

Recent Accounting Pronouncements to be Adopted

In May 2014, the FASB issued ASU 2014-09, "Revenue from Contracts with Customers (Topic 606)," which is a comprehensive new revenue recognition standard that will supersede existing revenue recognition guidance. The core principle of the guidance is that an entity should recognize revenue to depict the transfer of promised goods or services to customers in an amount that reflects the consideration to which the entity expects to be entitled in exchange for those goods or services. FASB issued ASU 2015-14 that deferred the effective date until annual periods beginning after December 15, 2018. Earlier adoption is permitted subject to certain limitations. The amendments in this update are required to be applied retrospectively to each prior reporting period presented or with the cumulative effect being recognized at the date of initial application. Management is currently evaluating the impact of this ASU on its financial statements.

In February 2016, the FASB issued ASU 2016-02, "Leases (Topic 842)," to increase transparency and comparability among organizations by recognizing lease assets and lease liabilities on the statement of financial position and disclosing key information about leasing arrangements for lessees and lessors. The new standard applies a right-of-use (ROU) model that requires, for all leases with a lease term of more than 12 months, an asset representing its right to use the underlying asset for the lease term and a liability to make lease payments to be recorded. The ASU is effective for fiscal years beginning after December 15, 2019 with early adoption permitted. Management is currently evaluating the impact of this ASU on its financial statements.

3. Income Taxes The Society has been granted tax-exempt status under Section 501(c)(6) of the Internal Revenue Code (IRC). The Society is required to report unrelated business income to the Internal Revenue Service. The Society had an insignificant amount of unrelated business income for the year ended December 31, 2016.

Example 3B

Society of Analysts and Affiliate

Notes to Consolidated Financial Statements

The Foundation has been granted tax-exempt status under Section 501(c)(3) of the IRC and has been classified as an organization that is not a private foundation under IRC Section 509(a). The Foundation had no unrelated business income for the year ended December 31, 2016.

Income tax benefits are recognized for income tax positions taken or expected to be taken in a tax return, only when it is determined that the income tax position will more likely than not be sustained upon examination by taxing authorities. The Organization has analyzed tax positions taken for filing with the Internal Revenue Service and all state jurisdictions where it operates. The Organization believes that income tax filing positions will be sustained upon examination and does not anticipate any adjustments that would result in a material adverse effect on the Organization's consolidated financial position, results of activities, or cash flows. Accordingly, the Organization has not recorded any reserves, or related accruals for interest and penalties for uncertain income tax positions at December 31, 2016. The Organization is still open to examination by taxing authorities for fiscal year 2013 and forward.

Example 3B

Society of Analysts and Affiliate

Notes to Consolidated Financial Statements

4. Contributions Receivable

The Foundation has a fundraising campaign to award scholarships to analysts for research projects.

Contributions receivable consists of unconditional promises to give as follows at:

December 31,	2016
Amounts receivable in:	
Less than one year	$ 79,645
One to five years	102,570
Total unconditional promises to give	182,215
Less: discount to net present value at rates ranging from 2.96% to 4.70%	(16,398)
Less: allowance for uncollectible contributions receivable	(44,125)
Net unconditional promises to give	121,692
Less: current portion	(79,645)
Noncurrent portion	$ 42,047

5. Fair Value Measurements

U.S. GAAP establishes a consistent framework for measuring fair value and expands disclosures for each major asset and liability category measured at fair value on either a recurring or nonrecurring basis. U.S. GAAP clarifies that fair value is an exit price, representing the amount expected to be received to sell an asset, or paid to transfer a liability, in an orderly transaction between market participants. As such, fair value is a market-based measurement that should be determined based on assumptions that market participants would use in pricing an asset or liability. To increase consistency and comparability in fair value measurements and related disclosures, U.S. GAAP sets forth a three-tier hierarchy for the inputs used to measure fair value based on the degree to which such inputs are observable in the marketplace, as follows:

Level 1: Valuation based on quoted prices in active markets for identical assets or liabilities that a reporting entity has the ability to access at the measurement date, and where transactions occur with sufficient frequency and volume to provide pricing information on an ongoing basis.

Example 3B

Society of Analysts and Affiliate

Notes to Consolidated Financial Statements

Level 2: Valuation based on inputs other than quoted prices included within Level 1 that are observable for the asset or liability, either directly or indirectly. Inputs include quoted prices for similar assets or liabilities in active markets, quoted prices for identical or similar assets or liabilities in markets that are not active, that is markets in which there are few transactions, prices are not current, or prices vary substantially over time.

Level 3: Valuation based on inputs that are unobservable for an asset or liability and shall be used to measure fair value to the extent that observable inputs are not available, thereby allowing for situations in which there is little, if any, market activity for the asset or liability at the measurement date. This input therefore reflects the Organization's assumptions about what market participants would use in pricing the asset or liability developed based on the best information available in the circumstances.

The Organization's investments in marketable securities (money market funds, equity mutual funds, and fixed income funds) are reported at fair value, based on quoted market prices. The fair value of the Organization's investments in marketable securities is determined to be Level 1 as they are traded in active markets.

The following table sets forth by level within the fair value hierarchy the Organization's investment assets and liabilities at fair value as of December 31, 2016. As required by U.S. GAAP, assets and liabilities are classified in their entirety based on the lowest level of input that is significant to the fair value measurement. The following table presents the Organization's investments that are measured at fair value on a recurring basis.

Investment Assets at Fair Value
as of December 31, 2016

	Level 1	Level 2	Level 3	Total
Investments:				
Equity Mutual Funds:				
U.S.-Blended	$ 2,552,165	$ -	$ -	$ 2,552,165
International Equity	2,416,953	-	-	2,416,953
U.S.-Large Cap Value	1,140,287	-	-	1,140,287
U.S.-Small Cap Value	545,894	-	-	545,894
U.S.-Small Cap Growth	112,259	-	-	112,259
Fixed Income Funds:	3,508,606	-	-	3,508,606
Money Market Funds:	132,767	-	-	132,767
Total investments at fair value	$ 10,408,931	$ -	$ -	$ 10,408,931

Example 3B

Society of Analysts and Affiliate

Notes to Consolidated Financial Statements

6. Property and Equipment

Property and equipment consists of the following at:

December 31,	2016
Furniture and equipment	$ 57,745
Computer equipment and software	1,809,897
	1,867,642
Less accumulated depreciation and amortization	(1,449,472)
Property and equipment, net	$ 418,170

Depreciation and amortization expense for the year ended December 31, 2016 was $415,334.

7. Line-of-Credit

During 2009, the Organization obtained a $500,000 line-of-credit with a financial institution. The interest on the line-of-credit is calculated at a variable rate of 1.5% over the LIBOR Market Index Rate. The interest rate as of December 31, 2016 was 2.40%. There was $475,000 outstanding on the lineof- credit at December 31, 2016. Any outstanding principal and accrued interest is due on demand. The line-of-credit expires August 14, 2018. The agreement requires the Organization to comply with certain financial and nonfinancial covenants.

8. Capital Leases

The Organization leases computer equipment under three separate capital leases expiring in the year 2018. The asset and liability under the capital leases is recorded at the lower of the present value of the minimum lease payments or the fair value of the assets. The assets are amortized over the lower of their related lease term or their estimated useful lives.

Amortization of the assets under the capital leases is included in depreciation and amortization expense for 2016. Following is a summary of the computer equipment held under capital leases at:

December 31,	2016
Computer equipment	$ 91,168
Less: allowance for amortization	(65,315)
	$ 25,853

Example 3B

Society of Analysts and Affiliate

Notes to Consolidated Financial Statements

Future minimum lease payments, by year and in the aggregate, under the capital leases are as follows at:

Year Ending December 31,

2017	$	20,843
2018		7,024
		27,867
Less: amount representing interest		(2,014)
Present value of future minimum lease payments		25,853
Less: current portion		(18,936)
Noncurrent capital lease obligation	$	6,917

9.   Net Assets with Donor Restrictions

Net assets with donor restrictions at December 31, 2016, are restricted for the following purpose or periods.

> Under ASU 2016-04 the underwater endowment amount is classified with net assets with donor restrictions instead of net assets without donor restrictions.

Time and purpose restricted:	
Contributions receivable due in future years for the purpose of providing scholarships for research	$ 121,692
Subtotal	121,692
Investment in Perpetuity:	
Subject to the Organization's endowment spending policy and appropriation:	
Continuing education program	2,240,855
Research	641,398
Underwater endowments	(200,620)
Total perpetual endowments	2,681,633
Total net assets with donor restrictions	$ 2,803,325

Example 3B

Society of Analysts and Affiliate

Notes to Consolidated Financial Statements

10. Board-Designated Net Assets

The Organization's Board has designated from net assets without donor restrictions $510,050 of net assets for the following purposes as of December 31, 2016.

Building reserve	$ 500,000
Quasi-endowment Research	10,050
	$ 510,050

11. Endowment

The Organization's endowment consists of the Analyst Endowment fundwhich consists of approximately 20 individual funds established for a variety of purposes. The endowment includes both donor-restricted endowment funds and funds without donor restrictions that have been designated by the Board to function as an endowment. As required by U.S. GAAP, net assets associated with endowment funds, including funds designated by the Board to function as endowments, are classified and reported based on the existence or absence of donor-imposed restrictions.

Example 3B

Society of Analysts and Affiliate

Notes to Consolidated Financial Statements

> Should indicate the name of the state when identifying the UPMIFA regulations in the footnote.

The Organization is subject to the Uniform Prudent Management of Institutional Funds Act (UPMIFA) and, thus, classifies amounts in its donorrestricted endowment funds as net assets with donor restrictions because those net assets are time restricted until the Board appropriates such amounts for expenditure. Most of those net assets also are subject to purpose restrictions that must be met before reclassifying those net assets to net assets without donor restrictions. The Board of the Organization has interpreted UPMIFA as not requiring the maintenance of purchasing power of the original gift amount contributed to an endowment fund, unless a donor stipulates to the contrary. As a result of this interpretation, when reviewing its donor-restricted endowment funds, the Organization considers a fund to be underwater if the fair value of the fund is less than the sum of (a) the original value of initial and subsequent gift amounts donated to the fund and (b) any accumulations to the fund that are required to be maintained in perpetuity in accordance with the direction of the applicable donor gift instrument. The Organization has interpreted UPMIFA to permit spending from underwater funds in accordance with the prudent measures required under the law. Additionally, in accordance with UPMIFA, the Organization considers the following factors in making a determination to appropriate or accumulate donor-restricted endowment funds:

(1) The duration and preservation of the fund,
(2) The purposes of the Organization and the donor-restricted endowment fund,
(3) General economic conditions,
(4) The possible effect of inflation and deflation,
(5) The expected total return from income and the appreciation of investments,
(6) Other resources of the Organization, and
(7) The investment policies of the Organization.

Example 3B

Society of Analysts and Affiliate

Notes to Consolidated Financial Statements

Endowment Net Asset Composition

The following table represents the composition of the Organization's endowment net assets by type of fund as of December 31, 2016:

	Without Donor Restrictions	With Donor Restrictions	Total
Board-designated endowment funds	$ 10,050	$ -	$ 10,050
Donor-restricted endowment funds			
Original donor-restricted gift amount and amounts required to be maintained in perpetuity by donor	-	2,411,633	2,411,633
Accumulated investment gains	-	270,000	270,000
Total funds	$ 10,050	$ 2,681,633	$ 2,691,683

Changes in Endowment Net Assets

The following table represents the changes in the Organization's endowment funds during the year ended:

December 31, 2016	Without Donor Restrictions	With Donor Restrictions	Total
Endowment net assets, beginning of the year	$ 9,645	$ 2,246,920	$ 2,256,565
Investment return, net	105	318,803	318,908
Contributions	-	200,000	200,000
Appropriation of endowment assets for expenditure	(200)	(84,090)	(84,290)
Other changes:			
Transfer to create board-designated endowment funds	500	-	500
Endowment net assets, end of year	$ 10,050	$ 2,681,633	$ 2,691,683

Example 3B

Society of Analysts and Affiliate

Notes to Consolidated Financial Statements

Underwater Endowment Funds

From time to time, the fair value of assets associated with individual donor-restricted endowment funds may fall below the level that the donor or UPMIFA requires the Organization to retain as a fund of perpetual duration. Deficiencies of this nature exist in five of the donor-restricted endowment funds, which together have an original gift value of $357,825, a current fair value of $157,205, and a deficiency of ($200,620) as of December 31, 2016. These deficiencies resulted from unfavorable market fluctuations that occurred shortly after the investment of new contributions for donor-restricted endowment funds and continued appropriation for certain programs that was deemed prudent by the Board.

Return Objectives and Risk Parameters

The Organization has adopted investment and spending policies for endowment assets that attempt to provide a predictable stream of funding to programs supported by its endowment while seeking to maintain the purchasing power of the endowment assets. Endowment assets include those assets of donor-restricted funds that the organization must hold in perpetuity or for a donor-specified period as well as board-designated funds. Under this policy, as approved by the Board, the endowment assets are invested in a manner that is intended to produce results that exceed the price and yield results of the S&P 500 index while assuming a moderate level of investment risk. The Organization expects its endowment funds, over time, to provide an average rate of return of approximately 8 percent annually. Actual returns in any given year may vary from this amount.

Strategies Employed for Achieving Objectives

To satisfy its long-term rate-of-return objectives, the Organization relies on a total return strategy in which investment returns are achieved through both capital appreciation (realized and unrealized) and current yield (interest and dividends). The Organization targets a diversified asset allocation that places a greater emphasis on equity-based investments to achieve its long-term return objectives within prudent risk constraints.

Example 3B

Society of Analysts and Affiliate

Notes to Consolidated Financial Statements

<u>Spending Policy and How the Investment Objectives Relate to Spending Policy</u>

The Organization has a policy of appropriating for distribution each year 5 percent of its endowment fund's average fair value over the prior 12 quarters through the calendar year-end preceding the fiscal year in which the distribution is planned. In establishing this policy, the Organization considered the longterm expected return on its endowment. Accordingly, over the long term, the Organization expects the current spending policy to allow its endowment to grow at an average of 3 percent annually. The Organization has a policy that permits spending from underwater endowment funds depending on the degree to which the fund is underwater, unless otherwise precluded by the donor intent or relevant laws and regulations.

12. Net Assets Released from Restrictions

Net assets were released from donor restrictions by incurring expenses satisfying the restricted purpose or by the occurrence of the passage of time or other events specified by donors as follows for the year ended December 31, 2016:

> This disclosure is optional but does increase the transparency to the reader regarding the release of restrictions.

Purpose restrictions accomplished:	
Investment return appropriated and released for current operations from donor-restricted endowments for continuing education program	$ 84,090
Satisfaction of time and purpose restrictions:	
Scholarships	100,078
Total restrictions released	$ 184,168

13. Description of Program and Supporting Services

The following program and supporting services are included in the consolidated statement of activities:

<u>Strategic marketing and communications</u>

Includes expenses incurred to further the Organization members' analyst services to the general public through specific marketing, education and media relations tactics. Also includes expenses for communicating current professional news to major media publications and Organization members.

Example 3B

Society of Analysts and Affiliate

Notes to Consolidated Financial Statements

Research and knowledge resources

Includes the costs of creating the Organization's member magazine. Also includes managing content on the Organization's website, editorial support services, and research services and the Foundation scholarship program.

Customer service

Responsible for assisting all members with any request or information via telephone, e-mail, or web.

Continuing education

The Organization offers a wide range of continuing education opportunities and knowledge of new techniques, products, important issues, and business management. These programs include workshops, lectures, and expenses related to the production and sale of educational materials.

Governance

Expenses cover costs relating to the governance structure of the Organization.

Finance and administration

Includes the functions necessary to maintain an adequate working environment and manage financial and budgetary responsibilities of the Organization.

Fundraising

Includes costs associated with the production of events, mailings, and general solicitations of funds for the Foundation.

Example 3B

Society of Analysts and Affiliate

Notes to Consolidated Financial Statements

14. Retirement Plan

The Organization maintains a 401(k) Profit Sharing Plan and Trust that covers substantially all full-time employees once they have reached age 21 and have completed six months of service. Under the terms of the plan, the Organization matches:

a. 100% of the participating employees' contribution up to 6% of the employees' salary; and
b. 50% of the participating employees' contribution for the next 2% of the employees' salary.

Contribution expense to the plan for the year ended December 31, 2016, was $113,882.

15. Commitments and Contingencies

Lease

The Organization leases space for its office under an operating lease that expires in December 2020. The lease includes certain pass-through occupancy expenses that are charged each year. The future minimum lease commitments under this lease, by year and in the aggregate, are as follows:

Year ending December 31,

2017	$ 130,000
2018	130,000
2019	130,000
2020	130,000
	$ 520,000

Rent expense for the year ended December 31, 2016 was $145,000.

Litigation

The Organization is subject to legal proceedings, claims, and liabilities which arise in the ordinary course of business. In the opinion of management, the amount of the ultimate liability with respect to those actions will not materially affect the Organization's consolidated financial position or cash flows.

Example 3B

Society of Analysts and Affiliate

Notes to Consolidated Financial Statements

16. **Related Party Transactions**

The Society performs various administrative tasks for the Foundation. The Society also provides office space and pays certain expenses on behalf of the Foundation and charges the Foundation for its share. The time and related salary for three Society staff members working on the Foundation is allocated to the Foundation and paid for from the Foundation budget.

17. **Departure From U.S. GAAP**

The Organization does not follow the generally accepted accounting principles that require recognition of the amount of contributed services as revenue and expenses in the consolidated financial statements. It was not practicable to determine the effects of the unrecorded contribution revenue and expenses on the consolidated financial statements.

18. **Subsequent Events**

The Organization has evaluated subsequent events through March 27, 2017, which is the date the consolidated financial statements were available to be issued.

There were no events noted that required adjustment to or disclosure in these consolidated financial statements.

Exercise 3B: Working with Financial Statements

Use the Society of Analysts and Affiliate consolidated financial statements in Example 3B to familiarize yourself with some of the concepts unique to nonprofit organizations.

1. Begin by looking at the independent auditor's report:
   a. What type of opinion is this?

   _____

   _____

   b. What period is covered by the report?

   _____

   _____

2. Locate the consolidated Statement of Financial Position:
   a. Locate the current and noncurrent portions of contributions receivable. Which footnote provides information on the components of contributions receivable? What is the net amount of contributions receivable?

   _____

   _____

   b. Locate noncurrent investments. Where can you find information on the types of investments held by the organization? What is the total amount of investments?

   _____

   _____

   c. What types of net assets does the organization have? What portion of net assets can be used to fund general operations?

   _____

   _____

   d. What is the total amount of net assets without donor restrictions?

   _____

   _____

   e. What is the current ratio (current assets/current liabilities) on December 31, 2016?

   _____

   _____

3. Locate the consolidated Statement of Activities:
   a. What is the total change in net assets without donor restrictions?

   _____

   _____

b. What is the total change in net assets with donor restrictions?

_____

_____

c. What amount of donor-restricted contributions was received during the year?

_____

_____

d. What is the total amount of net assets released from restrictions? What does this mean?

_____

_____

e. Did the organization's total operating revenues exceed operating expenses before net investment return?

_____

_____

4. Looking at the consolidated Statement of Functional Expenses:
   a. What is the largest natural expense incurred in the Finance and Administration supporting service category?

   _____

   _____

   b. What is the second-largest natural expense category overall?

   _____

   _____

5. Moving to the consolidated Statement of Cash Flows:
   a. What amount did the organization borrow on the line-of-credit during the year? In what section of the statement did you find this information?

   _____

   _____

   b. Did cash increase or decrease from FY 2015 to FY 2016?

   _____

   _____

6. Focusing on the footnotes:
   a. What does the organization consider a cash and cash equivalent?

   _____

   _____

b. How does the organization value its investments? Which footnotes can you get this information from?

_____

_____

c. What is the organization's capitalization policy for property and equipment?

_____

_____

d. What is the total amount of furniture and equipment the organization has? Which note contains this information?

_____

_____

e. Describe the Strategic Marketing and Communications program. Which note can this be found in?

_____

_____

7. Which components of the consolidated financial statements reflect the adoption of ASU 2016-14?

_____

_____

8. Among the most important issues revealed by the consolidated financial statements are the following:

_____

_____

Exercise 3B: Answers

1. Begin by looking at the independent auditor's report:

   a. What type of opinion is this?

   Modified as a result of a departure from generally accepted accounting principles.

   b. What period is covered by the report?

   Year ended December 31, 2016.

2. Locate the consolidated Statement of Financial Position:

   a. Locate the current and noncurrent portions of contributions receivable. Which footnote provides information on the components of contributions receivable? What is the net amount of contributions receivable?

   Note 4; $121,692.

   b. Locate noncurrent investments. Where can you find information on the types of investments held by the organization? What is the total amount of investments?

   Notes 2 and 5; $10,408,931.

   c. What types of net assets does the organization have? What portion of net assets can be used to fund general operations?

   With donor restrictions and without donor restrictions; without donor restrictions.

   d. What is the total amount of net assets without donor restrictions?

   $6,163,748.

   e. What is the current ratio (current assets/current liabilities) on December 31, 2016?

   The current ratio is .32, which is calculated by dividing current assets by current liabilities (905,108/2,800,266) and is considered a weak current ratio.

3. Locate the consolidated Statement of Activities:

   a. What is the total change in net assets without donor restrictions?

   $1,183,586.

   b. What is the total change in net assets with donor restrictions?

   $334,635.

   c. What amount of donor-restricted contributions was received during the year?

   $200,000.

   d. What is the total amount of net assets released from restrictions? What does this mean?

   $184,168 (Total of $84,090 and $100,078). These funds were spent in accordance with the donors' intention, or the time restriction has elapsed.

   e. Did the organization's total operating revenues exceed operating expenses before net investment return?

   Yes, by $606,878.

4. Looking at the consolidated Statement of Functional Expenses:
   a. What is the largest natural expense incurred in the Finance and Administration supporting service category?

   Salaries and wages, at $2,443,703.

   b. What is the second-largest natural expense category overall?

   Benefits and taxes, at $1,172,804.

5. Moving to the consolidated Statement of Cash Flows:
   a. What amount did the organization borrow on the line-of-credit during the year? In what section of the statement did you find this information?

   $475,000; cash flows from financing activities.

   b. Did cash increase or decrease from FY 2015 to FY 2016?

   Cash increased by $184,945.

6. Focusing on the footnotes:
   a. What does the organization consider a cash and cash equivalent?

   All highly liquid instruments with an original maturity of three months or less that are to be used for current operations, which excludes those held as part of the organization's long-term investments per Note 2, the Summary of Accounting Policies, under the Cash and Cash Equivalents heading.

   b. How does the organization value its investments? Which footnotes can you get this information from?

   At fair value; Note 2, Summary of Accounting Policies, under Investments, and Note 5.

   c. What is the organization's capitalization policy for property and equipment?

   The organization capitalizes assets with an original cost of $1,000 or greater per Note 2 under the Property and Equipment heading.

   d. What is the total amount of furniture and equipment that the organization has? Which note contains this information?

   $57,745; Note 6.

   e. Describe the Strategic Marketing and Communications program. Which note can this be found in?

   Specific marketing and media relations tactics are used to further the organization's members' analyst services to the general public; Note 13.

7. Which components of the consolidated financial statements reflect the adoption of ASU 2016-14?
   - *Change in terminology from unrestricted net assets to net assets without donor restrictions and from temporarily restricted and permanently restricted net assets to net assets with donor restrictions.*
   - *Liquidity and Availability disclosure in Note 2, Summary of Significant Accounting Policies (the entity had already included this before the adoption but other entities may not have).*

- *Functional allocation methodology for expenses is included in Note 2, Summary of Significant Accounting Policies.*
- *The effect of adopting ASU 2016-14 in Note 2, Summary of Significant Accounting Policies.*
- *The required analysis of expenses by function and nature was included as a separate basic financial statement titled, consolidated Statement of Functional Expenses.*
- *Note 9 was expanded to detail the nature of net assets with donor restrictions and present the components.*
- *Note 10 was added to detail the nature of board-designated net assets. (This note could be eliminated since the detail was shown on the face of the consolidated Statement of Financial Position, but was included here for illustrative purposes.)*
- *Note 11 was expanded and more detail was added related to the endowment funds to fully comply with ASU 2016-14.*
- *An Emphasis of a Matter paragraph was added to the independent auditor's report because of the change in presentation of underwater endowments required by ASU 2016-14 and the material effect of this change on the presentation of net assets without donor restrictions and net assets with donor restrictions.*

8. Among the most important issues revealed by the consolidated financial statements are the following:
   - *There are several important insights that the consolidated financial statements provide even though they are not comparative.*
   - *Based on a review of the consolidated Statement of Financial Position, you can note that current liabilities exceed the current assets by nearly triple. Although the organization holds mutual funds and other liquid investments in its portfolio, it would need to liquidate these assets if it needed cash for general operations. There may be losses that are realized if the assets needed to be liquidated in a down market. The organization may want to obtain professional investment advice on how to possibly structure some investments as liquid assets that may not have the potential for a loss if it needed to liquidate these quickly.*
   - *As noted in the consolidated Statement of Financial Position, the organization also owes $475,000 on its line-of-credit. The line-of-credit is used to offset timing differences between when the cash is received and when amounts are due. The membership dues are paid based on a September 30 due date, so there are often times when cash is needed throughout the year to smooth this out. The organization is incurring interest expenses on these borrowings and should analyze this cost in comparison to the potential to restructure the investments as noted earlier to try to smooth out these fluctuations at the lowest possible cost.*
   - *What is clear from the Statement of Activities is that the organization's single-largest source of revenue is membership dues. This comprises 60 percent of the total revenue. The organization may want to consider plans to further diversify its revenue streams to provide against future declines that could occur from dues. You would need to look at prior year financial statements to see the full picture of the trend in dues revenue.*
   - *Based on looking at the consolidated Statement of Activities, you can also see that finance and administration costs of $4,000,738 nearly equal total program costs of $4,515,682. The organization is incurring an inordinate amount of overhead costs to run the operations. Further investigation needs to be performed on this anomaly.*

CHAPTER 21

Financial Analysis

Preparing accurate and timely financial information is the goal of every financial system. Whether you have one part-time bookkeeper or a dozen accountants providing this information, it is critical to the health and welfare of your organization. It is, however, only the first step. The information developed is valuable only if it is used, and the better use you make of it, the more value you and your organization receive. The task in financial analysis is to make optimal use of the available financial information by extracting from it the organizational insight it contains.

The type of financial analysis required is best done by senior management or senior financial personnel since we are talking about deciding what the key numbers are and how they have changed over the preceding months or years. The financial expertise the organization relies on, whether staff professionals (in the mid-size and larger organizations) or volunteer leaders (in the smaller ones) should communicate these critical insights clearly and concisely.

This information could include not only important information from the financial statements and important nonfinancial activity, but also data derived from analytical procedures such as industry standards or your organization's historical benchmarks.

At a minimum, such financial analysis information should include:

1. What is the state of the organization's key indicators? (Health of critical revenue, and so forth.)
2. What are the important financial changes you should be made aware of? Which are positive and which are negative? (Change in net assets, and so forth.)
3. Are there related items whose trends should be considered?

It is then up to you to see if these insights warrant further investigation, or some sort of action. It is your job to make sure that you are receiving the information you need to manage and provide oversight to your organization successfully.

Ratio Analysis

There are different forms of ratio analysis that can be used when examining an entity's financial information. The following list gives a few different options for performing a ratio analysis.

1. Insight into an organization's financial information can be substantially improved by looking at one number from the financial statements in relation to one or more other numbers. These relationships, or ratios, are generally expressed as a percentage (100 percent) or as a formula ("1:1" meaning "1 to 1").
2. Ratios generally fit into various categories including liquidity, profitability, operating efficiency, and leverage. The following ratios listed are a selection of those that are typically useful in analyzing nonprofit organizations.

Indicator	Significance	If High[1]	If Low[2]
Statement of Financial Position/Balance Sheet			
Total revenue/ total assets	Ability to maximize use of assets to create income and measure of operating efficiency.	Organization is optimizing the use of its assets (desirable).	Organization is operating inefficiently.
Current assets/ current liabilities	Ability to pay obligations when due (shorter term).	May appear too rich to members or other resource providers.	Organization may not have the ability to pay its bills on time.
Cash and investments/deferred revenue	Extent to which current resources may be attributable to next year's income.	Organization is not relying on future income.	Organization may be spending next year's income.
Total liabilities/ total net assets	Extent to which activities have been financed by borrowing.	Organization may not be earning enough from operations.	Normally a desirable situation; however, organization may be losing opportunities.
Statement of Activities/Income Statement			
(Total revenue– total expense)/ total revenue	Whether organization is (1) living within its means or (2) maximizing its program services.	Organization may appear too rich and may not be maximizing its program services.	If deficits continue, organization may be in financial difficulty.
Program service expenses/total expenses[3]	Extent to which activities directly benefit members of the organization.	Normally a desirable situation.	Overhead may be excessive, or organization may be new, troubled, or controversial.
Membership dues/ total expenses[4]	Reliance on income generated by dues.	Organization may lack diversity in its revenue streams.	Organization may reduce its focus on member needs.

Indicator	Significance	If High[1]	If Low[2]
Other Nonprofit Specific Ratios			
Total contributions (excluding government grants)/fundraising expense	Measure the relative cost and efficiency to produce voluntary contributions from the general public.	Normally a good indicator.	Fundraising efforts may not be very efficient.
General and administrative expenses/total expenses	Measure the efficiency of the use of general support raised from unrestricted contributions in relation to overall activities.	Organization may need to evaluate its general and administrative expenses.	Organization is efficient or organization may not be appropriately investing in its infrastructure.

[1] As noted earlier, for most financial indicators, it is not possible to define standard, desirable, or average values because of a scarcity of data, and considering the variety of organizations in the not-for-profit sector. The columns, "If High" and "If Low" are provided to help users consider what would be appropriate levels for a particular organization at a particular time. For example, an organization that provides disaster relief whenever tragedy or natural disasters strike clearly needs more operating reserves than does an organization not subject to large, unpredictable, immediate demands on its resources (that is, when the Big One hits).

[2] See preceding footnote.

[3] This indicator is one of the most widely used—and overused—indicators in the not-for-profit sector. While it is not unimportant and is certainly worth looking at, many people ascribe too much weight to this in assessing organization performance—which often translates into, "Will I support this organization?" An organization that spends, say, 80 cents (inputs) on programs (outputs) out of every dollar it spends is not necessarily doing more good for its stakeholders than one that spends only 70 percent. One must consider the quality and effectiveness of what they are doing (outcomes). Tracking ratios like these over time is probably a more effective use of the indicators, as is making sure that you (management, board member, fundraiser, and so forth), are always prepared to reply to a skeptical questioner as to why your ratio is such-and-such, for example, not as good (at least in the eyes of the questioner) as the comparable ratio of that other nonprofit over there.

[4] This ratio can be used to analyze any revenue stream.

3. Relevant Comparative Ratios
   a. The best comparative ratios are the historical ones for a particular nonprofit organization. By comparing the entity to its past performance, a trend line can be developed that will highlight the variances and situations that should be investigated.
   b. Comparative figures in the nonprofit industry are difficult to use effectively given the extraordinary diversity of size, method of operation, and purpose of these entities. Nevertheless, a variety of ratios and comparative figures are available from industry sources. This is discussed in more depth in the benchmarking section.
4. Specialized Ratios
   Every organization will have peculiarities of its own that can be highlighted to aid management. The following is a list of some relationships others have used to analyze components of their organization:
   a. Annual event revenue versus annual event expense
   b. Pages of advertising versus total publication pages

Going Beyond the Ratios

Although using financial ratio analysis can highlight important information about an organization, these measures are only one-dimensional. To move beyond this, many organizations are also providing quantitative information about how effective the organization is at achieving its goals. An example of this would be to not only present the ratio analysis related to overhead costs, they will also report the number of activities performed, or the increase in the number of members served in a given time period. The closer an organization's measures align with the organization's mission and goals, the more meaningful they can be. For example, if an organization provides low-interest loans to businesses, then information about the number of loans and their repayment rates may be critical indicators of the organization's success.

Some of this information could be incorporated into the organization's financial statements to convey this message and the success of the organization to its readers. The nonprofit industry has not embraced the use of a section titled "Management's Discussion and Analysis" as a foreword to the financial statements that discusses from management's viewpoint, the successes and struggles of the organization, and provides the story behind the numbers that readers will see in the financial statements themselves. The use of this is an option that is exercised by a few organizations and should be considered by others.

The ability of an organization to tell its story to the readers of the financial statements is critical. There continues to be increased competition for financial resources that can affect the ability of the organization to deliver their programmatic activities. There has been a significant decline in funding received from state and local governments, as well as the federal government, in recent years. At the same time the need for many of the services offered by nonprofit organizations has increased. Organizations are continually faced with trying to balance the need to find money to meet the increased demand from communities and individuals to whom they provide their services.

This need to find alternative sources of funds requires that organizations need to compete for these resources. In order to do so, organizations need to be transparent about their finances, outcomes, and results. Donors, as well as funders, want to know how their money is being spent. Through the use of data visualization, such as infographics and other such tools, organizations show how they are meeting their programmatic objectives, outcomes, and missions. Using pictures and graphics to tell a story is becoming more popular.

CHAPTER 22

Benchmarking

Many organization volunteers and executives are interested in determining whether their organization is positioned as well, or performing as well, as it should be. To make this assessment, they generally want to compare their organization to other similar organizations or to industry standards. This type of comparison is called benchmarking, which is another form of financial analysis.

Benchmarking started in the for-profit world in response to a need on the part of decision makers to optimize their decisions. Can you use these techniques in the nonprofit sector as well? Yes—to a point. Some of the benchmarks used by for-profits carry over into the nonprofit sector. Some do not, and there are others that have meaning to nonprofits that would not be used in for-profits.

Profitability, while measurable for a nonprofit in the same way, takes on a whole different meaning in our sector. Since, by definition, we do not have owners who are seeking a personal financial return from their involvement with us, one question to ask is, who cares how much profit we make?

What is success in a nonprofit organization? This is the fundamental question. In the for-profit world, success is generally measured by profit—often referred to as the bottom line. A for-profit entity that makes a profit is considered successful because it can use that profit for some combination of payout to the owners and reinvestment in the company to make it grow and earn even more profits in the future.

But how do you define, much less measure, success in the nonprofit sector? Clearly, the "excess of revenue over expenses" is not it, although this number does provide us with some useful information. For example, it tells whether we have lived within our means during the year—that is, did we spend more than we took in, or did we take in more than we spent?

Another way to say this is, are we better or worse off financially than we were at the beginning of the year? Large, continuing deficits almost certainly foreshadow a financial crisis, which, if not dealt with, will likely mean the end of the organization. So this indicator can be an early warning sign of impending trouble.

On the other hand, large excesses of revenue do lead to financial health—which is good, but may have downsides as well. For example, if a membership organization gets to be very financially healthy, it is likely to run into member resistance to paying dues.

A member or donor, seeing that the organization already has sizable financial resources, may inquire, "Why are you asking me for more money? Spend what you have!" Or the organization's employees may seek a raise in pay.

The following statement describes an additional downside: "Every dollar that hits our bottom line is a dollar that was not spent in achieving our program mission." Many board members and donors get uncomfortable when contemplating this thought.

Most meaningful measures of success in the nonprofit sector are based on program accomplishments, but we must be careful. It is easy to get misled into thinking that, say, a nonprofit's success can be measured by statistics such as the number of people who attend the annual meeting, participate in a program or buy publications. And, while I will grant that many nonprofit organizations that are generally considered excellent score well against such benchmarks, these are not necessarily true measures of success.

We must keep in mind the difference between inputs, outputs, and outcomes:

- Inputs are things such as the number of dollars spent on a program. Staff salaries and facility costs also fall in this group. But those are not measures of success. Those are things that, if wisely used, help achieve success.
- Outputs are things like the number of meetings held, number of participants in a program, or books published. These are measures of quantities of something, but are not measures of success, although we are getting closer.

What we really would like to know is the amount of knowledge and analytical ability possessed by those using our outputs, and how well they will now be able to use that knowledge and ability to better accomplish their goals or those of the organizations they represent. Those are outcomes, the true measure of a success for a nonprofit.

The problem with nonprofits is that it is often very difficult to accurately define, much less measure, outcomes. Another problem is that many outcomes can only be meaningfully determined over lengthy periods of time. So we tend to fall back on other benchmarks—such as outputs or inputs—as surrogates for outcomes.

Types of Benchmarking

So, are there financial benchmarks that are useful for nonprofits? Yes, although there is not the widespread acceptance of a particular body of benchmarks that there is in the for-profit world. It is important to be aware that, for many of the benchmarks used by nonprofits, it is generally quite difficult to define "standard," "desirable," or even "average" values because of a general scarcity of useful data and to the great variability of types, sizes, and operating characteristics of organizations in the nonprofit sector. Given these concerns, most experts in the field recommend that an organization develop comparisons based on their own historical performance.

Another option is to look at other relevant organizations in your industry to develop a more precise set of comparative figures. These can be developed by gathering data for specific, similar organizations. It is not uncommon for a group of organizations that do not compete, but do business in similar fields, and operate similarly, to share their financial information. Because these groups are often in the same physical area, another possible cause of lack of comparability can be eliminated.

The most valuable insight, however, can be gained by benchmarking against the performance of the organization itself.

CHAPTER 23

Increasing Complexity in Nonprofit Financial Reporting

New Pronouncements Affecting Nonprofit Financial Statements

The Financial Accounting Standards Board (FASB) has issued several Accounting Standards Updates (ASU) that affect the preparation of nonprofit financial statements. A major effect of these pronouncements is an increase in the amount of information that needs to be included in the footnotes to provide expanded information to the reader and increase the transparency of the numbers included in the financial statements. Users of financial statements are being provided with more and more information, but the user needs to understand the additional information provided to be able to draw accurate conclusions regarding the entity.

The effective dates noted here are based on the effective date of these ASUs for nonpublic entities. Certain ASUs consider nonprofit organizations that have issued, or are a conduit bond obligor (that is, holder of certain limited-obligation revenue bonds or similar debt instruments issued by a state or local governmental entity), of securities that are traded, listed, or quoted on an exchange or over-the-counter market to be subject to the effective date established for public business entities. If an organization meets the definition of a public business entity in the specific ASU, they may need to adjust the effective dates of these requirements to those for a public business entity. Generally, the effective dates will be a year earlier for public business entities. Please refer to the actual ASU for the full information on effective dates.

ASU 2014-09, *Revenue from Contracts with Customers (Topic 606)*

In May 2014, the FASB issued ASU 2014-09, *Revenue from Contracts with Customers (Topic 606)*, which is a comprehensive new revenue recognition standard that will supersede existing revenue recognition guidance. The core principle of the guidance is that an entity should recognize revenue to depict the transfer of promised goods or services to customers in an amount that reflects the consideration to which the entity expects to be entitled in exchange for those goods or services. FASB issued ASU 2015-14 that deferred the effective date of ASU 2014-09 until annual periods beginning after December 15, 2018. Earlier adoption is permitted subject to certain limitations. The amendments in this update are required to be applied retrospectively to each prior reporting period presented or with the cumulative effect being recognized at the date of initial application.

ASU 2014-15, Presentation of Financial Statements—Going Concern (Subtopic 205–40): Disclosures of Uncertainties about an Entity's Ability to Continue as a Going Concern

In August 2014, the FASB issued ASU 2014-15, *Presentation of Financial Statements–Going Concern (Subtopic 205-40): Disclosures of Uncertainties about an Entity's Ability to Continue as a Going Concern*. The update provides guidance about management's responsibility to evaluate whether there is substantial doubt about an entity's ability to continue as a going concern. The update also provides related disclosures. The guidance is effective for annual periods ending after December 15, 2016.

ASU 2015-07, Fair Value (Topic 820), Disclosures for Investments in Certain Entities that Calculate Net Asset Value per Share (or Equivalent)

In May 2015, the FASB issued ASU 2015-07, *Fair Value (Topic 820), Disclosures for Investments in Certain Entities that Calculate Net Asset Value per Share (or Equivalent)*, which allows for those entities that have elected the practical expedient to use the net asset value (NAV) as a measure of fair value and to no longer categorize these investments within the fair value hierarchy. The practical expedient criteria differ from the criteria used to categorize other fair value measurements within the hierarchy. A reporting entity should continue to disclose information on investments for which fair value is measured at NAV (or its equivalent) as a practical expedient to help users understand the nature and risks of the investments and whether the investments, if sold, are probable of being sold at amounts different from NAV. The ASU is effective for fiscal years beginning after December 15, 2016, with early application permitted and should be applied retrospectively. The retrospective approach requires that an investment for which fair value is measured using the NAV practical expedient be removed from the fair value hierarchy in all periods presented in an entity's financial statements.

ASU 2016-02, Leases (Topic 842)

In February 2016, the FASB issued ASU 2016-02, *Leases (Topic 842)*, to increase transparency and comparability among organizations by recognizing lease assets and lease liabilities on the statement of financial position (balance sheet) and disclosing key information about leasing arrangements for lessees and lessors. The new standard applies a right-of-use (ROU) model that requires, for all leases with a lease term of more than 12 months, an asset representing its right to use the underlying asset for the lease term and a liability to make lease payments to be recorded. The ASU is effective for fiscal years beginning after December 15, 2019, with early adoption permitted.

ASU 2016-14, Not-for-Profit Entities (Topic 958): Presentation of Financial Statements of Not-for-Profit Entities

In August 2016, the FASB issued ASU 2016-14, *Not-for-Profit Entities (Topic 958): Presentation of Financial Statements of Not-for-Profit Entities*. The ASU amends the current reporting model for nonprofit organizations and enhances their required disclosures. The major changes include: (a) requiring the presentation of only two classes of net assets now titled "net assets without donor restrictions" and "net assets with donor restrictions," (b) modifying the presentation of underwater endowment funds and related disclosures, (c) requiring the use of the placed-in-service approach to recognize the expirations of restrictions on gifts used to acquire or construct long-lived assets absent explicit donor stipulations otherwise, (d) requiring that all nonprofits present an analysis of expenses by function and nature in either the statement of activities, a separate statement, or in the notes and disclose a summary of the allocation methods used to allocate costs, (e) requiring the disclosure of quantitative and qualitative information regarding liquidity and availability of resources, (f) presenting investment return net of external and direct internal investment expenses, and (g) modifying other financial statement reporting requirements and disclosures intended to increase the usefulness of nonprofit financial statements. The ASU is effective for the financial statements for fiscal years beginning after December 15, 2017. Early adoption is permitted. The provisions of the ASU must be applied on a retrospective basis for all years presented although certain optional practical expedients are available for periods presented before the adoption of the ASU.

Other Changes on the Horizon

Phase 2 of FASB's Project on Nonprofit Financial Statements

When the FASB was developing ASU 2016-14, there were certain issues that were moved to Phase 2 of the project that needed more time to be addressed based on the feedback from constituents. The items that were moved to Phase 2 of this project were:

Operating Measure
- Should there be a requirement to present an operating measure in nonprofit financial statements?
- Whether and how to define such operating measures and what items should be included.

- Alignment of measures of operations in the statement of activities with measures of operations in the statement of cash flows.

As of the date of this publication, there wasn't a stated time frame for the completion of Phase 2 of the project. If you want to stay abreast of any discussions related to the topics in Phase 2, you can access this on the FASB website at www.fasb.org.

Revenue Recognition of Grants and Contracts by Not-for-Profit Entities

The FASB has added a project entitled "Revenue Recognition of Grants and Contracts by Not-for-Profit Entities" to their agenda. This project was added to address the difficulty and diversity in practice for recognizing revenue from grants and contracts for not-for-profit entities that stem from the following two issues:

Issue 1: How NFPs characterize grants and similar contracts with government agencies and others as (1) reciprocal transactions (exchanges) or (2) nonreciprocal transactions (contributions).

Issue 2: Distinguishing between conditions and restrictions for nonreciprocal transactions.

This project is in process and once resolved the outcome will impact how these transactions are recorded.

CHAPTER 24

Nonprofits Subject to *Government Auditing Standards* and a Single Audit under the Uniform Guidance

The Single Audit Act and the *Uniform Administrative Requirements, Cost Principles, and Audit Requirements for Federal Awards* (Uniform Guidance, or UG) requires a non-federal entity (including nonprofit organizations) that expends $750,000 or more of federal awards in a fiscal year to have a single or program-specific audit. The Single Audit Act and the UG require independent external auditors to perform single audit and program-specific audits of federal awards in accordance with *Government Auditing Standards*.

In December 2013, the Office of Management and Budget (OMB) issued Title 2 Code of Federal Regulations (CFR) Part 200, *Uniform Administrative Requirements, Cost Principles, and Audit Requirements for Federal Awards* that established uniform cost principles and audit requirements for federal awards expended by nonfederal entities, and administrative requirements for all federal grants and cooperative agreements. This guidance consolidated the requirements from OMB Circulars A-21, A-87, A-89, A-102, A-110, A-122, and A-133. Subpart A of the UG outlines the acronyms and definitions used in the UG. Subparts B through D of the UG set forth the uniform administrative requirements for grants and cooperative agreements. Subpart E establishes principles for determining the allowable costs incurred by nonfederal entities under federal awards. Subpart F sets forth standards for obtaining consistency and uniformity among federal agencies for the audit of nonfederal entities expending federal awards. Federal awarding agencies may apply subparts A through E of the UG to for-profit entities, foreign public entities, or foreign organizations.

The requirements in Subpart F, "Audit Requirements," of the UG are effective for audits of fiscal years beginning on or after December 26, 2014. Therefore, auditees who are subject to a single audit for fiscal years ended December 25, 2015 or later will be required to undergo the audit under the UG audit requirements. Early implementation of the Subpart F guidance was not permitted. Under the Subpart F provisions of the UG, changes in the single audit process include an increased audit threshold from $500,000 to $750,000 in annual federal expenditures (unless total federal expenditures exceed $25 million) and an increased threshold for reportable questioned costs from $10,000 to $25,000. Other changes to the single audit were made and organizations with federal funding should refer to the Uniform Guidance at www.ecfr.gov for more information.

The cost principles and administrative requirements defined under the UG are effective for all federal awards and certain funding increments provided on or after December 26, 2014. The effective date provisions mean that an auditor will be required to use the cost principles and administrative requirements found in the individual circulars for awards and funding increments awarded before December 26, 2014, and to use the UG cost principles and administrative requirements for federal awards and certain funding increments awarded on or after December 26, 2014. Going forward, depending on the award dates of the nonfederal entity's federal awards, an auditor may be required to use both of these sources of guidance while performing the compliance audit of federal awards because some federal awards are subject to the pre-UG requirements (those awarded before December 26, 2014), while other federal awards are subject to the cost principles and administrative requirements of the UG (those awarded on or after December 26, 2014). The effective date provisions of the UG cost principles and administrative requirements are not affected by whether the audit is performed under OMB Circular A-133 or the UG audit requirements.

Key changes in the administrative requirements per the UG include: increased monitoring and management processes over subrecipients; enhanced documentation requirements over procurement procedures and the establishment of five procurement methods that must be followed; and increased documentation over the establishment and maintenance of internal controls over the federal awards that provides reasonable assurance that the nonfederal agencies are managing the federal awards in compliance with federal statutes, regulations, and the terms and conditions of the federal awards.

An organization has the option to issue a separate set of financial statements that report only on the standard audited financial statements that will appear exactly as the examples that we have provided previously. If an organization opts to issue only one reporting package that includes both the standard report on the audited financial statements and the reports required by the Uniform Guidance and *Government Auditing Standards,* however, there will be certain differences.

- The first item to note is the independent auditor's report on the financial statements will be much longer since this will also address the requirements of *Government Auditing Standards.* A sample report that would be issued under *Government Auditing Standards* with an unmodified or clean opinion is shown further on in this chapter. This sample report also includes the auditor's opinion on the supplemental schedule of expenditures of federal awards (SEFA). The auditor's opinion on the SEFA, however, may be included in the independent auditor's report on compliance with requirements applicable to each major federal program and on internal control over compliance in accordance with the Uniform Guidance instead of the auditor's report on the financial statements.

The full single audit reporting package would contain the following reports:

- Independent auditor's report on the financial statements
- Independent auditor's report on internal control over financial reporting and on compliance and other matters based on an audit of financial statements performed in accordance with *Government Auditing Standards*
- Independent auditor's report on compliance with requirements applicable to each major federal program and on internal control over compliance in accordance with the Uniform Guidance
- Schedule of expenditures of federal awards and the notes to the schedule
- Schedule of findings and questioned costs
- Summary schedule of prior audit findings (if necessary)
- Corrective action plan (if necessary)

Sample Unmodified Independent Auditor's Report Issued on Basic Financial Statements of a Nonprofit Nongovernmental Entity Accompanied by Other Information in Accordance with *Government Auditing Standards*

Report on the Financial Statements

We have audited the accompanying financial statements of the Nonprofit Organization (the "Organization"), which comprise the statement of financial position as of December 31, 2016, and the related statements of activities and cash flows for the year then ended, and the related notes to the financial statements.

Management's Responsibility for the Financial Statements

Management is responsible for the preparation and fair presentation of these financial statements in accordance with accounting principles generally accepted in the United States of America; this includes the design, implementation, and maintenance of internal control relevant to the preparation and fair presentation of financial statements that are free from material misstatement, whether due to fraud or error.

Auditor's Responsibility

Our responsibility is to express an opinion on these financial statements based on our audits. We conducted our audits in accordance with auditing standards generally

(continued)

(continued)

accepted in the United States of America and the standards applicable to financial audits contained in *Government Auditing Standards,* issued by the Comptroller General of the United States. Those standards require that we plan and perform the audit to obtain reasonable assurance about whether the financial statements are free from material misstatement.

An audit involves performing procedures to obtain audit evidence about the amounts and disclosures in the financial statements. The procedures selected depend on the auditor's judgment, including the assessment of the risks of material misstatement of the financial statements, whether due to fraud or error. In making those risk assessments, the auditor considers internal control relevant to the entity's preparation and fair presentation of the financial statements in order to design audit procedures that are appropriate in the circumstances, but not for the purpose of expressing an opinion on the effectiveness of the entity's internal control. Accordingly, we express no such opinion. An audit also includes evaluating the appropriateness of accounting policies used and the reasonableness of significant accounting estimates made by management, as well as evaluating the overall presentation of the financial statements.

We believe that the audit evidence we have obtained is sufficient and appropriate to provide a basis for our audit opinion.

Opinion

In our opinion, the financial statements referred to above present fairly, in all material respects, the financial position of the Organization as of December 31, 2016, and the changes in its net assets and its cash flows for the year then ended in accordance with accounting principles generally accepted in the United States of America.

Other Matters

Other Information

Our audit was conducted for the purpose of forming an opinion on the financial statements as a whole. The accompanying schedule of expenditures of federal awards, as required by Title 2 U.S. Code of Federal Regulations (CFR) Part 200, *Uniform Administrative Requirements, Cost Principles, and Audit Requirements for Federal Awards* (Uniform Guidance) is presented for purposes of additional analysis and is not a required part of the financial statements. Such information is the responsibility of management and was derived from and relates directly to the underlying accounting and other records used to prepare the financial statements. The information has been subjected to the auditing procedures applied in the audit of the financial statements and certain additional procedures, including comparing and reconciling such information directly to the underlying accounting and other records used to prepare the financial statements or to the financial statements

(continued)

(*continued*)

themselves, and other additional procedures in accordance with auditing standards generally accepted in the United States of America. In our opinion, the information is fairly stated, in all material respects, in relation to the financial statements as a whole.

Other Reporting Required by Government Auditing Standards

In accordance with *Government Auditing Standards,* we have also issued our report dated March 7, XXXX on our consideration of the Organization's internal control over financial reporting and on our tests of its compliance with certain provisions of laws, regulations, contracts, and grant agreements and other matters. The purpose of that report is to describe the scope of our testing of internal control over financial reporting and compliance and the results of that testing, and not to provide an opinion on internal control over financial reporting or on compliance. That report is an integral part of an audit performed in accordance with *Government Auditing Standards* in considering the Organization's internal control over financial reporting and compliance.

March 7, XXXX

GLOSSARY
PRIOR TO EFFECTIVE DATE OF ASU 2016-14

The terms included in the glossary are common terms that are encountered in discussions of nonprofit financial statements and general accounting terms used in discussions involving nonprofit business activities. Many of these terms appear in nonprofit financial statements and these definitions will help readers understand the terms.

The items marked with an asterisk (*) are either replaced by new terms or the definitions have been modified as noted in the section titled "Glossary: Amendments Made Upon Adoption of ASU 2016-14." These definitions become effective for the entity once they adopt ASU 2016-14.

The definitions marked with this symbol (†) are based on the Financial Accounting Standards Board (FASB) Accounting Standards Codification (ASC) Master Glossary.

account The smallest subcategory in which financial activity is tracked. Thus, an account is a specific item of asset, liability, net asset, revenue, or expense. Also, a section of a general ledger in which only the financial activity of that particular item is recorded.

account balance The net difference between total debits and credits posted to an account.

accounts payable An amount owed to an outside party for goods or services received.

accounts receivable An amount owed to the organization from another party for goods and services sold by the organization on credit.

accrual basis accounting A method of accounting based on the economic reality of a transaction. Thus, revenues are reflected in the accounts when earned rather than when payment is received, and expenses are recorded in the accounting period incurred, rather than when paid. Although more complicated than cash-basis accounting, accrual-basis accounting results in a better matching of revenues with the expenses incurred to generate those revenues.

accrued expense/accrued liability Expenses incurred in one accounting period that will be paid for in a subsequent accounting period. Similar in nature to an accounts payable, but tend to be internally generated expenses, for example, accrued salary.

amortization Similar to depreciation in that it is a method of allocating the cost of an asset over the period in which the asset is used. Most often applied to leasehold improvements and intangible assets rather than fixed assets such as furniture and buildings.

assets   Items of economic value owned by an organization.

board–designated endowment fund*†   An endowment fund created by a not-for-profit entity's (NFP's) governing board by designating a portion of its unrestricted net assets to be invested to provide income for a long but unspecified period (sometimes called *funds functioning as endowment* or *quasi-endowment funds*). (See *endowment fund*.) (See also *designated net assets*.)

change in net assets   See *net income and/or net loss*.

contribution†   An unconditional transfer of cash or other assets to an entity, or a settlement of debt that is voluntary and nonreciprocal.

current asset   Cash or other assets expected to be converted into cash within one year of the reporting period. Examples: cash held in checking accounts and accounts receivable due within one year of the reporting period.

current liability   An obligation due to be paid within one year of the reporting period. Example: accounts payable.

deferred revenue   See *unearned revenue*.

depreciation expense   Annual allocation of a portion of the original cost of a fixed asset to expense over the asset's estimated useful life.

designated net assets*†   Unrestricted net assets subject to self-imposed limits by action of the governing board. Designated net assets may be earmarked for future programs, investment, contingencies, purchase or construction of fixed assets, or other uses.

donor–imposed restriction*†   A donor stipulation that specifies a use for the contributed asset that is more specific than broad limits resulting from all of the following:

a. The nature of the not-for-profit entity (NFP)
b. The environment in which it operates
c. The purposes specified in its articles of incorporation or bylaws, or comparable documents for an unincorporated association.

A donor-imposed restriction on an NFP's use of the asset contributed may be temporary or permanent. Some donor-imposed restrictions impose limits that are permanent, for example, stipulating that resources be invested in perpetuity (not used up). Others are temporary, for example, stipulating that resources may be used only after a specified date, for particular programs or services, or to acquire buildings and equipment.

donor–restricted endowment fund*†   An endowment fund that is created by a donor stipulation requiring investment of the gift in perpetuity or for a specified term. Some donors may require that a portion of income, gains, or both be added to the gift and invested subject to similar restrictions. The term does not include a board-designated endowment fund. (See *endowment fund*.)

endowment fund*† An established fund of cash, securities, or other assets to provide income for the maintenance of an NFP. The use of the assets of the fund may be permanently restricted, temporarily restricted, or unrestricted. Endowment funds are generally established by donor-restricted gifts and bequests to provide either of the following: (a) a permanent endowment, which is to provide a permanent source of income, or (b) a term endowment, which is to provide income for a specified period. Alternatively, an NFP's governing board may earmark a portion of its unrestricted net assets as a board-designated endowment fund.

expense Cost of assets used up and liabilities incurred for the purpose of earning revenues.

fiscal year Twelve-month accounting period selected by an organization. It may be calendar year-end, or end on any other month-end.

functional classification*† A method of grouping expenses according to the purpose for which costs are incurred. The primary functional classifications are program services and supporting activities.

fundraising† Activities undertaken to induce potential donors to contribute money, securities, services, materials, facilities, other assets, or time. Fundraising expenses are supporting services.

funds functioning as endowment*† Unrestricted net assets designated by an entity's governing board, rather than restricted by a donor or other outside agency, to be invested to provide income for a long but unspecified period. A board-designated endowment, which results from an internal designation, is not donor-restricted and is classified as unrestricted net assets. The governing board has the right to decide at any time to expend the principal of such funds. (Sometimes referred to as quasi-endowment funds.) (See also *designated net assets*.)

furniture and equipment A part of fixed assets. Tangible property, usually with a long useful life, used in the revenue-producing activities of the organization.

investments Assets held for production of income that is incidental to the main operations and programs of the organization. Example: investment in bonds and stocks that earn interest and dividends.

liability An obligation owed for goods or services received in the past that will be paid at a future time.

long-term liability A liability that is expected to be paid at a future time greater than one year from the reporting period. Example: the long-term portion of a mortgage payable.

management and general activities*† Supporting activities that are not identifiable with a single program, fundraising activity, or membership-development activity but that are indispensable to the conduct of those activities and to an entity's existence.

natural expense classification*† A method of grouping expenses according to the kinds of economic benefits received in incurring those expenses. Examples of natural expense classifications include salaries and wages, employee benefits, supplies, rent, and utilities.

net assets*† Residual value of an organization after liabilities have been paid (Assets less Liabilities = Net Assets). Sometimes called *net equity*. There are three mutually exclusive classes of net assets depending on the existence or absence of donor-imposed restrictions: unrestricted net assets, temporarily restricted net assets, and permanently restricted net assets.

net income (change in net assets) Excess of revenues over expenses (previously called *profit*).

net loss or deficit (change in net assets) Excess of expenses over revenues. A net loss is frequently shown in brackets ($xxx).

permanently restricted net assets*† The portion of an organization's net assets resulting from contributions of assets whose use by the organization is limited by donor-imposed stipulations that neither expire by the passage of time nor can be fulfilled or otherwise removed by actions of the organization.

prepaid expense Advance payment of a cost that will provide benefits over a future time. Example: prepaid insurance.

program services† Activities that result in goods and services being distributed to beneficiaries, customers, or members that fulfill the purposes or mission of the organization.

realized gain/loss The amount that results from the sale of an asset. If the organization's cost exceeds the sales price, the result will be a loss incurred by the organization. If the cost is less than the sales price, the result will be a gain. (See *unrealized gain/loss*.)

reclassifications*† Simultaneous increase of one class of net assets and decrease of another, usually as a result of the release or lapsing of restrictions.

restricted support† Donor-restricted revenues or gains from contributions that increase either temporarily restricted net assets or permanently restricted net assets. Monies received by a not-for-profit by grant or donation that are explicitly limited by the donor as to how they may be used. Restrictions vary; a contribution might be limited to use for a specific project, for a specific time period, or it might be limited in that only income earned on the contribution may be spent.

revenue The value of what is received in exchange for goods sold or services provided.

Statement of Activities One of the basic financial statements. It summarizes the revenues and gains generated and expenses and losses incurred during the accounting period in question and results in a change in net assets (net income or net loss).

Statement of Financial Position (or Balance Sheet) One of the basic financial statements; it shows at a particular date the economic worth of a nonprofit. The statement reflects the assets owned by the organization, the liabilities owed by the organization, and the residual net assets (representing the net worth).

supporting activities[†] Activities, other than program services, consisting primarily of management and general, fundraising, and membership-development activities.

temporarily restricted net assets[*†] The part of net assets resulting from contributions of assets whose use by the organization is limited by donor-imposed stipulations that either expire by the passage of time or can be fulfilled and removed by actions of the organization pursuant to those stipulations.

unearned revenue Also called *deferred revenue*. A liability based on advance payment by another party for goods or services the nonprofit will provide in the future.

unrealized gains/loss The difference between the fair value of an asset being held and its total cost at a certain point in time.

unrestricted net assets[*†] The part of net assets of an NFP that is neither permanently restricted nor temporarily restricted by donor-imposed stipulations. The only limits on the use of unrestricted net assets are the broad limits resulting from the following:

a. The nature of the NFP
b. The environment in which the NFP operates
c. The purposes specified in the NFP's articles of incorporation or bylaws and
d. Limits resulting from contractual agreements with suppliers, creditors, and others entered into by the NFP in the course of its business.

voluntary health and welfare entities[†] An NFP that is formed for the purpose of performing voluntary services for various segments of society and that is tax exempt (organized for the benefit of the public), supported by the public, and operated on a not-for-profit basis. Most voluntary health and welfare entities concentrate their efforts and expend their resources in an attempt to solve health and welfare problems of our society and, in many cases, those of specific individuals. As a group, voluntary health and welfare entities include those NFPs that derive their revenue primarily from voluntary contributions from the general public to be used for general or specific purposes connected with health, welfare, or community services. For purposes of this definition, the general public excludes governmental entities when determining whether an NFP is a voluntary health and welfare entity.

GLOSSARY
AMENDMENTS MADE UPON ADOPTION OF ASU 2016-14

All of these definitions are based on the Financial Accounting Standards Board (FASB) Accounting Standards Codification (ASC) Master Glossary.

board-designated endowment fund An endowment fund created by a not-for-profit entity's (NFP's) governing board by designating a portion of its net assets without donor restrictions to be invested to provide income for a long but not necessarily specified period (sometimes called *funds functioning as endowment* or *quasi-endowment funds*). In rare circumstances, a board-designated endowment fund also can include a portion of net assets with donor restrictions. For example, if an NFP is unable to spend donor-restricted contributions in the near term, then the board sometimes considers the long-term investment of these funds. (See *endowment fund*.)

board-designated net assets Net assets without donor restrictions subject to self-imposed limits by action of the governing board. Board-designated net assets may be earmarked for future programs, investment, contingencies, purchase or construction of fixed assets, or other uses. Some governing boards may delegate designation decisions to internal management. Such designations are considered to be included in board-designated net assets.

donor-imposed restriction A donor stipulation (donors include other types of contributors, including makers of certain grants) that specifies a use for a contributed asset that is more specific than broad limits resulting from the following:

a. The nature of the not-for-profit entity (NFP)
b. The environment in which it operates
c. The purposes specified in its articles of incorporation or bylaws or comparable documents for an unincorporated association.

Some donors impose restrictions that are temporary in nature, for example, stipulating that resources be used after a specified date, for particular programs or services, or to acquire buildings or equipment. Other donors impose restrictions that are perpetual in nature, for example, stipulating that resources be maintained in perpetuity. Laws may extend those limits to investment returns from those resources and to other enhancements (diminishments) of those resources. Thus, those laws extend donor-imposed restrictions.

donor-restricted endowment fund An endowment fund that is created by a donor stipulation (donors include other types of contributors, including makers of certain grants) requiring investment of the gift in perpetuity or for a specified term. Some donors or laws may require that a portion of income, gains, or both be added to the gift and invested subject to similar restrictions. The term does not include a board-designated endowment fund. (See *endowment fund*.)

donor-restricted support Donor-restricted revenues or gains from contributions that increase net assets with donor restrictions (donors include other types of contributors, including makers of certain grants).

endowment fund An established fund of cash, securities, or other assets to provide income for the maintenance of a not-for-profit entity. The use of the assets of the fund may be with or without donor-imposed restrictions. Endowment funds generally are established by donor-restricted gifts and bequests to provide a source of income in perpetuity or for a specified period. (See *donor-restricted endowment fund*.) Alternatively, an NFP's governing board may earmark a portion of its net assets as a board-designated endowment fund. (See *funds functioning as endowment*.)

functional expense classification A method of grouping expenses according to the purpose for which costs are incurred. The primary functional classifications of a not-for-profit entity are program services and supporting activities.

funds functioning as endowment Net assets without donor restrictions (donors include other types of contributors, including makers of certain grants) designated by an entity's governing board to be invested to provide income for generally a long but not necessarily specified period. A board-designated endowment, which results from an internal designation, is generally not donor-restricted and is classified as net assets without donor restrictions. The governing board has the right to decide at any time to expend such funds. In rare circumstances, funds functioning as endowment also can include a portion of net assets with donor restrictions. For example, if an NFP is unable to spend donor-restricted contributions in the near term, the board sometimes considers the long-term investment of these funds. (Sometimes referred to as quasi-endowment funds or board-designated endowment funds.) (See *board-designated endowment fund*.)

management and general activities Supporting activities that are not directly identifiable with one or more program, fundraising, or membership-development activities.

natural expense classification A method of grouping expenses according to the kinds of economic benefits received in incurring those expenses. Examples of natural expense classifications include salaries and wages, employee benefits, professional services, supplies, interest expense, rent, utilities, and depreciation.

net assets The excess or deficiency of assets over liabilities of a not-for-profit entity which is divided into two mutually exclusive classes according to the existence or absence of donor-imposed restrictions. (See *net assets with donor restrictions* and *net assets without donor restrictions*.)

net assets with donor restrictions   The part of net assets of a not-for-profit entity that is subject to donor-imposed restrictions (donors include other types of contributors, including makers of certain grants).

net assets without donor restrictions   The part of net assets of a not-for-profit entity that is not subject to donor-imposed restrictions (donors include other types of contributors, including makers of certain grants).

programmatic investing   The activity of making loans or other investments that are directed at carrying out a not-for-profit entity's purpose for existence rather than investing in the general production of income or appreciation of an asset (for example, total return investing). An example of programmatic investing is a loan made to lower-income individuals to promote home ownership.

reclassification of net assets   The simultaneous increase of one class of net assets and decrease of another. A reclassification of net assets usually results from a donor-imposed restriction (donors include other types of contributors, including makers of certain grants) being satisfied or otherwise lapsing.

underwater endowment fund   A donor-restricted endowment fund for which the fair value of the fund at the reporting date is less than either the original gift amount or the amount required to be maintained by the donor or by law that extends donor restrictions.

ABOUT THE AUTHORS

Andrew S. Lang is president of LangCPA Consulting, a firm located in Potomac, Maryland and specializing in the nonprofit industry. He is recognized industry-wide for more than 40 years' experience serving a variety of nongovernmental nonprofit organizations, including foundations, associations, and charitable organizations. Andrew previously served as BDO (Binder Dijker Otte) USA's national director of nonprofit services.

Andrew is an accomplished writer, penning many articles and texts including *Financial Responsibilities of Nonprofit Boards*, Second Edition and *Understanding Nonprofit Financial Statements*, Second Edition.

In 2009, he began a three-year term on the board of governors of the Greater Washington Society of Certified Public Accountants. He is the immediate past president and chair of its ethics committee.

He completed 11 years on the American Institute of Certified Public Accountants' (AICPA) annual not-for-profit industry conference planning committee, serving as chairman during the final three. He served on the AICPA governmental and not-for-profit expert panel and the American Society of Association Executives' (ASAE) finance and business operations section council. He was also named ASAE's first associate member fellow in finance.

Andrew received a BS from the University of Wisconsin. He was a teaching fellow at Johns Hopkins University, where he earned his MFA, and an adjunct professor at American University.

William Eisig is the Atlantic Managing Partner of BDO USA, LLP and Executive Director of the BDO Institute for Nonprofit Excellence^{SM} with nearly 30 years of experience in public accounting. As Atlantic Managing Partner he oversees 10 BDO offices. Bill also sits on the board of directors at BDO USA, LLP.

A *SmartCEO* magazine CPA Innovator of the Year, Bill has extensive experience advising tax-exempt organizations on all phases of financial and compliance audits, internal controls, and policies and audit plans and programs.

He is a member of many groups, including the American Society of Association Executives (ASAE), the Greater Washington Board of Trade board of directors, the Greater Washington Society of Certified Public Accountants, the Maryland Association of Certified Public Accountants, and the American Institute of Certified Public Accountants, serving as BDO's representative for the governmental audit quality center.

He previously collaborated with the ASAE as a co-author of *Association Audits from A to Z.*

A former board president for the Montgomery County Chamber of Commerce, Bill holds a seat on the advisory board of the Robert Smith School of Business at the University of Maryland, where he earned a BS in accounting.

Lee Klumpp is the National Nonprofit & Eduction Industry Group Audit and Accounting Technical Director. Lee is an industry veteran with more than two decades of experience working with and advising organizations in the nonprofit and government sectors on accounting, auditing, governance, and finance issues, and is a major contributor to BDO's Institute for Nonprofit Excellence^{SM}.

Lee recently completed a fellowship with the Financial Accounting Standards Board (FASB), where he worked on several projects that affect the nonprofit industry, including Accounting Standards Update 2016-14, and remains a member of their nonprofit resource group.

Lee is a frequent speaker at various professional conferences and seminars on not-for-profit and government accounting issues. Lee also acts as a national instructor for nonprofit and governmental accounting and auditing topics at the American Institute of Certified Public Accountants (AICPA). Lee has also served on several committees of the AICPA, including the ethics committee's technical standards subcommittee, the guide to effective audit committees for nonprofit organizations task force, the not-for-profit revenue recognition task force and the state and local government independence task force. He is currently the treasurer of the Greater Washington Society of CPAs (GWSCPA) and the treasurer of the Congressional Awards Foundation. He previously served as the GWSCPA's not-for-profit committee chairman and has held various positions on other nonprofit boards.

Lee received a BS in accounting from the University of Maryland.

Tammy Ricciardella is a director in BDO's Institute for Nonprofit Excellence^{SM} and has more than 30 years of accounting experience providing assurance services to a variety of nonprofit clients, including associations, membership organizations, charitable organizations, foundations, and health and welfare organizations. Her role in the Institute is to provide technical insights both to BDO professionals and their clients.

She previously served as chief financial officer of a technology company and interim chief financial officer of National 4-H Council.

Tammy is the editor of BDO's quarterly nonprofit and education industry Group newsletter, *Nonprofit Standard,* and she authored BDO's *Guide to Effective Audit Committees for Nonprofit Organizations.*

She is a member of the American Institute of Certified Public Accountants (AICPA) and has taught technical courses for organizations such as AICPA, the American Society of Association Executives, and the Greater Washington Society of CPAs.

Tammy also develops and teaches various internal and external technical training courses on various topics, including fraud risk; effective audit committees; and various OMB Circular A-133, Uniform Guidance, and Yellow Book topics.

She holds a BS in accounting from the University of Maryland.

BDO Institute for Nonprofit Excellence^{SM}

BDO's Institute for Nonprofit Excellence^{SM} (the Institute) has the skills and knowledge to provide high-quality services and address the needs of the nation's nonprofit sector. Based in our Greater Washington, DC metro office, the Institute supports and collaborates with BDO offices around the country and the BDO international network to develop innovative and practical accounting and operational strategies for the tax-exempt organizations they serve. The Institute also serves as a resource, studying and disseminating information pertaining to nonprofit accounting and business management. For more information, please visit: www.bdo.com.

INDEX